John,
Happy c
Trails always'.
Josie

Grab Your Tails
and
Ride the Trails

© Copyright 1997
Second Edition

By Josie Rusho and Rene Ogan

Josie Rusho / Rene Ogan

Printed by:	The Craftsman
Photography:	Rusho/Ogan
Maps:	Rusho/Ogan/Johnson/Ross Ogan
Illustrations:	Rusho/Ogan
Published By:	Horse of Course
Formatting/Editing:	Graham Nott/Lori Gray

Finally, a book that I've always longed for. To touch the hearts and souls of the people searching for ways to enjoy our forests on horseback, I will share with you lush valleys, steep canyons and refreshing meadows, from my hoofprints to yours.

Happy Trails,
Josie Rusho

From the past many years on horseback. To the future many more years with family and friends taking solitide on high ridgetops, listening to nature's own sounds on the backs of our beloved stock, who take us places we'd never reach otherwise. I hope others experience that peaceful feeling of accomplishment after a day in the saddle from dawn to dusk!
Rene Ogan

Acknowledgments

We'd like to express thanks to our husbands, Cliff and Greg, and to our boys, Nick, Ross, Greg and Corey, for the patience they've had while we were gone during the years of riding hundreds of miles of trails and during the time it took to put this book together. We spent many evenings with our heads buried in paper and maps!

Sincere thanks to our veterinarian, Dr. Paula J. Thompson for contributing her knowledge on trail emergencies. To our farriers, Jack Wallace and Don Hampton for keeping shoes on our stock, even at 5:00 a.m.! To Graham Nott and Lori Gray for editing and helping in the transition from manuscript to book. To all the folks at Jerrol's Bookstore and to The Copy Shop in Ellensburg for all the helpful advice. To Ray at Sagebrush Saddlery, Ellensburg Saddle Company, and Donny Bacon for repairs on our tack.

In Washington State, the Cle Elum and Leavenworth Ranger Districts and the Kittitas County Sheriff ORV and Search and Rescue Departments have supported our efforts in putting this book together. In Oregon State, the Sisters and Bend Ranger Districts were helpful in reviewing our manuscript.

Take Heed with Your Steed

Animals have a mind of their own and can be unpredictable in any situation. They have the "Fight or Flight" instinct. We've presented basic guidelines and information that may help you make sound decisions and reduce risk. This book covers several potential hazards that you could encounter and that should be dealt with according to an individual's skill and experience. Know your and your horse's limits before you hit the trail. Use good sensible judgment and be responsible for your own actions and decisions. Safety is your responsibility. Take it seriously! We thank you for taking heed. Clear streams and high mountains to ya!

"Saddle Up!"

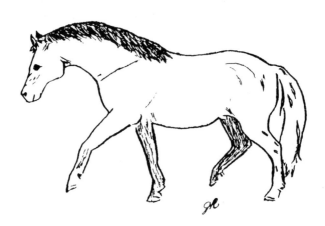

Table of Contents

Introduction

Well, the unexpected has happened because almost eight years ago neither of us ever thought of writing a trail book! What better way to express our love for horses and the mountains. We have such a desire to share our exciting experiences of all these years in the hills with you.

We took the big step, jumped in with both feet and put this book together to guide you on these trails.

We rode each trail described in this book and learned from experience how to deal with unique situations by reading maps and challenging ourselves with different circumstances. Plan, prepare and know your own limits. We recommend riding with someone compatible and choosing stock depending on the rider's ability.

We met each other years ago in an exercise class and know the importance of personal physical conditioning as an integral part of enjoying and appreciating that 30-mile ride.

We've included Eastern Washington, the North Cascades down to Central Oregon's Three Sisters area because we're both explorers by nature. With as much riding as we've done, after riding a trail both directions several times, we find it's time to move on and explore new trails! We really appreciate these two states' versatile geography. There are so many different types of trails to enjoy without venturing too far.

In our trail descriptions, we give an overall picture rather than a detailed account, because we feel strongly that individuals should discover the solitude and majestic presence of the wilderness on their own.

Our Rating System

- **EASY:** flat, wide trail, possibly a few rocky areas and slight elevation changes.

- **MEDIUM:** climbing, drop-offs, open hillsides or rocky spots.

- **HARD:** difficult terrain, steep climbing, cliffs, poor footing on narrow hillsides and obstacles in the trail.

We've used a combination of these ratings followed by the reasons for two ratings, e.g., Easy-Medium (climbing). What may be an Easy trail to one could quite possibly be a Medium-Hard trail to another. We've put a lot of thought into our ratings and feel that the trails are rated as fair as possible. Remember that each year trail conditions change due to severe weather. Check with local rangers for current trail and road conditions and always travel prepared for the unexpected.

Maps

Green Trails Maps (GTM)

We use Green Trails Maps when we ride on the trail. They can be purchased at Jerrol's Bookstore in Ellensburg or directly from Green Trails: P.O. Box 77734, Seattle, WA 98177, (206) 546-6277.

A North Central Cascades map and others are available from R. A. Pargeter, P.O. Box 844, Kent, WA 98031. These maps have a 3D effect and are very interesting to read.

Other more detailed topographical maps can be used. Contact the Forest Service for wilderness maps in Washington and Oregon. We do recommend the use and comparison of several different current maps. We have discovered discrepancies. Use updated maps!

Wilderness

To ensure stockmen will be welcomed into wilderness areas in the future, we need to follow certain guidelines. Always phone local Ranger Stations to get current information that may effect your trip. Also, let them know about problems you encounter or things that were great, such as trail improvements. When you register at the trailheads, there is a comment, suggestions area... fill it in!

In Washington State, group size is limited to 12 beating hearts, including people and stock combined. For other arrangements and permits, check with local rangers. In Oregon State, they allow 12 people plus 12 horses in a group. They are considering going to a 12 beating hearts policy. Various wildernesses have their own group size limits.

Keep stock 200' away from water sources to preserve water purity and shoreline vegetation. The use of hobbles, highlines and other containment is a must! (Hobble stock that paw immediately.) We recommend tree savers when using highlines. Where time regulations exist, tying to a tree is limited to 30-60 minutes without hobbling. Use only processed stock feed to avoid the spreading of noxious weeds and move stock frequently when picketing to avoid overgrazing.

Read your maps...
Sometimes the
wilderness
is just that!

Check on campfire use and restrictions, and use camp stoves when possible. In the Alpine Lakes Wilderness, campfires are prohibited above 5000' east of the Cascade Crest and above 4000' west of the Cascade Crest. A word from the Forest Service, "Please don't smoke in the hills."

Motorized equipment, such as chain saws, are not allowed in wilderness areas. Only emergency situations involving the Sheriff's Office and Forest Service allow for such equipment use. Leaving equipment or supplies unattended for more than 48 hours is prohibited in particular areas.

U-pack it in, U-pack it out!! Use lightweight equipment and dried, prepackaged food when possible. Earth tones are a lot more pleasing to see in the mountains than a bright pink tent! Take all cans and aluminum foil home. A good practice to get into is always taking the time to pick up garbage when you see it.

Use designated camps where required, e.g., hiker or horse. Keep camps away from water sources, and in a spot with minimal impact. Place tents in a previously used area, rather than in a new spot. Scatter manure before you leave and fill in any holes. Our motto is: "Always leave camp cleaner than you found it!"

Tread lightly, don't cut switchbacks, and preserve our wilderness areas. We recommend staying single file on trails and if you are compelled to ride off trail, spread out... This keeps new social trails from starting. Complying with these and all regulations will help ensure stock usage and will benefit us all.

Trailwise - Tread Lightly

Horse and pack animals have the right of way when meeting hikers or bikes. Ask them to step to the downside of the trail. Asking a hiker a question, "How are you today?" will get folks to speak easier than requesting them to "say something". Stock can recognize a voice. A moving backpack atop a silent hiker can be quite scary! We always thank others for yielding.

Maintained trails usually have a name or number. Expect to see one of these and in addition, you may also run across a yellow, square metal marker with a hole punched out. This is a township marker; you'll need a map with township squares marked on it to coincide with this. Sometimes in wilderness situations, you need to navigate to find sections of the trail. Watch for rock cairns, tree blazes and other significant trail signs: a rock cairn is a piling of rocks; a blaze out of the bark of a tree signifies a trail; numbers or letters included in the trail number are spur sections of a main trail. Letters and numbers refer to the same trail, e.g., Trail 456.A is the same as 456.1., 456.B is the same as 456.2. We abbreviate Green Trails Map as GTM, and Pacific Crest National Scenic Trail as PCT.

Dig those "cat holes" at least 200 feet away from creeks, lakes, camp and the trails...

If you lose the trail, which happens in some meadows, search the rim of the meadow for signs signifying continuation of it. Map reading comes in handy when you need to count creek crossings and study terrain. Always carry a compass and learn how to use it!

Shortcuts usually are not the designated trail! Switchbacks are used to reduce the grade of the land and prevent erosion. Brush and branches across one of two trail choices means that one is now closed and has been re-routed. Waterbars are the half-buried logs placed diagonally across the trails to divert the water. Have your stock go straight through puddles to keep these areas small. This keeps the edges dry for those on foot and prevents widening of the trail.

When crossing water, aim upstream and give the stock full use of the head and neck. If dismounted, stay downstream from the animals, so as not to drift into the swimming legs and hooves. People sometimes experience dizziness while crossing rivers, so look upstream or elsewhere, not downstream. Cross in wide areas with no swirling current. These areas could have submerged obstacles or be deep pools.

Turning around on a steep, narrow spot can be quite a challenge. Stay calm and have your animal's front end turn to the outside.

Crossing snow can be treacherous. Judge the time of year, condition, angle and depth of snow. The experience of horse and rider should be considered. You may want to lead your horse to lessen the weight or send the horse on its own. Be safe and use good judgment.

The ability to deal with whatever comes along on the trail takes calmness, sensibility and willingness of all involved. Ride with compatible people and stock for a pleasant outing. Some like to walk; some trot all day. Some enjoy the forest; some crave the ridgetops. Compassion is needed when riding with young, inexperienced stock and novice riders. Find a good riding partner.

Trail Tack

Well-fitted tack is a must. Check with your saddlemaker for possible problem spots. The only dry area after a ride should be right down the spine. Sometimes more padding causes more pressure. Breastcollars and breaching or cruppers are helpful. These keep the saddle centered on the stock's back. If a flank cinch is used, it should be kept snug and attached to the front cinch. Clean, well-fitted tack is of the utmost importance. Old leather and loose screws could bring some unwanted and dangerous surprises in the hills. We have snaps on both of our reins in case we need a quick release.

Trail Clothing and Weather

No matter what time of year you're riding, always prepare for the unexpected weather. Layer natural fabrics, carry dry wool socks in a Ziplock bag, protect yourself from too much sun and always have a coat and rain gear (plastic garbage bags work well). We recommend dressing in earth tones to reduce visual impact to other visitors.

Mother Nature can be quite sneaky at times. Always be aware of your surroundings and take notice of subtle changes around you. Quick changes in wind patterns, erratic campfire smoke and distant thunder are all changes to be aware of. Lightning strikes sharp cliff areas more frequently than smooth areas. If you are in a lightning storm, tie up your animals, find a dry spot and crouch with both feet together. Respect Mother Nature, know what to do in poor weather situations and prepare before you leave home.

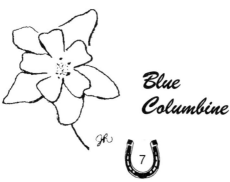

Blue
Columbine

Packing Tips

Safety is the first priority. Having a fantastic trip is second. For tying, learn the basic diamond hitch and its variations. The use of half-hitches in the stocks' tails to lead up a string of pack animals can be very effective; breakaway ropes are a good choice too. In some situations, you need to let them individually pick their own way. Emergency use of antlers and horseshoes on cinches for lash hooks and rings is a lifesaver. Practice hobbling, picketing, etc., at home first. Picketing by the front foot, not the halter, is much safer. Check all pack gear rigging prior to your trip. A balanced load is probably the most important task. We like to carry a hand-held meat scale to weigh out the packs. Your stock will travel easier and longer! You'll learn the most by doing and by asking old-timers their packing tips. Use folding canvas water buckets as they can also double as feed bags. U-pack it in, U-pack it out. Carrying a cross-cut saw enables you to clear trails as you ride. The Forest Service sure appreciates the help!

Pack Food Ideas

The length of the trip determines what type of food to bring. On shorter trips, we bring lightweight, prepackaged foods. On the longer trips, we tend to load up on canned goods and start out with steaks! The hearty food sure tastes good after a week in the hills.

- Catch fresh fish, where allowed
- Frozen steaks, hamburgers, chicken (eat these first)
- Chili, spaghetti, soups, pork 'n beans, potatoes
- Canned vegetables, fruits, sauces
- Oatmeal, packaged noodles, mac 'n cheese
- Pancake mix, bread, bagels, crackers, cereals
- Canned juices, candy bars,
    cookies, dried fruit
- Eggs: Pack carefully.
    Use 2 bottoms of egg cartons
    together with paper towels to pad.

Black Morel

8

Supplies (Truck and Trailer)

Truck: Extra supplies brought are oil, fuses, flashlight with extra bulb and batteries, jack, spare tire for truck and trailer, duct tape, electrical tape, tool box, jumper cables, rake, garbage bags, shovel, axe, flares, wood blocks. A C.B. radio comes in handy where there is active logging.

Trailer: We carry enough tack to completely outfit a horse twice. Bucket, dry bran in a Ziplock bag, mineral oil, brushes, hoofpicks, coats, gloves, socks, hat, shoes, 5 gallons of water, insect repellent, sponge, horse blanket, easyboots, leg wrapping, electrolytes, saddle bags and first aid kits for you and your stock. Always have your trailer checked over thoroughly each spring. Accidents can be prevented. Check flooring boards under the mats for any signs of rotting and lift the mats during the winter to let the floor air out. Think safety; use your own judgment.

First aid and survival kit (person): Anti-inflammatory, smelling salts, suture needle and thread, Band-Aids and wrap, water, throat lozenges, space blanket, scissors, high protein bars, waterproof matches and a lighter, water purifying tabs or filter, anti-histamines, allergy medication, Tea Tree oil (good insect repellent and antiseptic), cleansing agent, knife, compass, maps, whistle, signal mirror, large plastic bag (water collection, rain gear), sun screen, sun glasses and a warm hat and gloves.

Horse Kit: Bute tablets (paste), electrolytes, leg wraps, wound dressing and spray, tape and any other helpful items. Insect repellent (helps prevent pawing).

Saddle bags: Safety kits, water, hay pellets, foldup hand saw, extra rope, easyboot and hoofpick. We always have extra food and clothing during the ride and back at camp. A gun with extra shells should be carried on your person in case you need to put stock down, signal for help or use for survival. Other essential tools are a knife, a leather awl, and compass.

Emergency Situations

In an emergency, remember three of any type of signal means HELP! Venturing into remote destinations on horseback is a thrill to us all. Recognizing common equine emergency situations will help you to assess and provide needed treatment. Get with your veterinarian to review basic procedures of first aid to your stock.

Supplies:

- Bute
- Topical antibiotic (furacin)
- Insect repellent
- Bandage/wrap materials
- Scissors
- Hoofpick

Some common emergencies

- Colic
- Heat Stroke and Dehydration
- Snake Bites
- Thumps
- Tying up
- Founder (laminitis)
- Wounds/Bleeding
- Ocular (eye) emergencies

Trail Emergencies (and Treatments)

It is important in an emergency to know basic information on what a normal horse's body functions are. A normal temperature is 99-101.5 degrees, normal pulse rates are 28-40 beats per minute and normal resting respiration is 8-16 breaths per minute. The last two are easily calculated by counting them for 15 seconds and multiplying by four. The pulse is taken at the arteries located inside the jaw, inside of the knee of the foreleg and at the back of the fetlock joints. Respiration is observed by stepping back and counting the movements of the ribs as each breath is taken. Temperature is taken with a heavy-gauge rectal thermometer.

- **COLIC:** Colic refers to abdominal pain. There are several types in stock:

1. Flatulent: The most common is caused by gas, and often is the most violent, with a lot of pain. It is also the least serious. Symptoms include quiet spells and painful spells. Pulse is usually not above 50.

2. Obstructive: Caused by an obstruction of food or feces that blocks the bowel. Symptoms are constant pain, the animal may paw, and the pulse usually is in the 60's.

3. Twist: The most serious kind is when the bowel is twisted. It can be fatal even with surgical intervention. Symptoms include a pulse rate in the 80's, constant pain and violent thrashing and rolling. Remember these are guidelines and individual horses may not show severe pain or raised pulse with a serious colic, while another horse may be very painful with a simple colic. Since the layman cannot judge how serious the condition may be, evaluation by a veterinarian is recommended.

Treatment:
1. Control pain to prevent rolling and twisting of intestines and injury to the horse (and you!). Potent tranquilizers and pain killers may be needed, which can only be provided by a veterinarian.

2. Treatment for suspected causes of colic. Mineral oils can be given orally for flatulent and obstructive colic to help move ingesta through the digestive system. Be careful the horse does not aspirate the mineral oil into the lungs, since severe pneumonia can develop. Bran mashes can be given. Be sure to walk the horse and keep him from rolling. Remove feed and provide water. Return to feed gradually, using leafy grass hay. Twist colic requires evaluation by a veterinarian.

- **HEATSTROKE AND DEHYDRATION:** These can be caused by poor conditioning and over-exertion in hot weather. This combination depletes energy and fluids. Symptoms:

1. Weakness

2. Lack of willingness to continue

3. Elevated pulse, respiration and temperature rising to 110 degrees

4. No longer sweating

5. Skin slowly retracts when pinched

6. No thirst or appetite

Treatment:
1. Cool down with water on the lower part of the legs, thighs, head and neck; never on the back.
2. Add 1-2 grams of Phenylbutazone (bute) per 1000 lbs. of horse every 12 hours.
3. Rest, water and electrolytes are recommended for the horse.
4. Call your veterinarian if there are no signs of improvement in 30 minutes.

- **SNAKE BITES:** Most commonly, horses are bitten by snakes on the head and neck. Symptoms include:

   1. Rapid swelling

   2. Difficulty in breathing

   3. Oozing dark blood and serum from the wound area. This would be a key sign in distinguishing a snake bite from a bee sting.

Treatment:

   1. Call your veterinarian.

   2. Apply a tourniquet 15 minutes at a time above the bite area if it's on an extremity.

   3. Apply cold packs to the area to reduce swelling, but don't use ice or frozen packs as they can damage tissue. Also note the time when the bite occurred. Prognosis: There is a 70-90% chance of recovery.

- **THUMPS:** The causes of thumps include hot climate, electrolyte imbalance and over-working. The symptoms are fatigue and a diaphragm contraction, which is synchronized with the heart rate and is seen as a twitch in the flank and is heard as thumping.

Treatment:

   1. Make sure the horse rests.

   2. Call your veterinarian.

   3. Give electrolytes using an empty and clean syringe; mix powder with water and give like wormer.

   4. Provide access to water.

- **TYING UP (AZOTURIA):** Tying up is caused by giving a horse a high nutritional diet while not exercising him. It usually affects a very fit horse which is returned to work after a layoff during which its' feed has not been reduced. This is also referred to as "Monday morning disease." Symptoms include:

1. Sore muscles 10-30 minutes after the ride has begun.

2. Stiffness and copious sweating.

3. Pain and coffee-colored urine.

Treatment:

1. Call your veterinarian.

2. Cover loosely with hot blankets, over the loins, if possible.

3. Rest the horse; let him stand, don't move him.

4. Give Phenylbutazone to reduce the pain and a tranquilizer to reduce anxiety. The veterinarian can prescribe an antihistamine, cortisone, Butazolidin, rest and a special diet.

Prognosis: Most horses which receive proper treatment completely recover. It is very important that the horse is not walked since further muscle and kidney damage can occur and the horse could die.

Prevention: When the horse is not working, cut back the feed and eliminate the grain! Josie had a personal experience with this in the desert of Nevada while conditioning for an endurance race and almost lost her horse due to ignorance.

- **FOUNDER (LAMINITIS):** Laminitis means inflammation of the laminae which attaches the hoofwall to the coffin bone. The inflammation can lead to the destruction of the laminae and rotation of the coffin bone down to the sole. If founder is untreated, it may cause permanent lameness or death. Severe cases may need corrective shoes to prevent further rotation of the coffin bone.

Cause:
1. Sudden dietary changes to the rich feed (overgrazing on grass pastures)

2. Allergy

3. Excessive, unaccustomed ingestion of grain

4. Mare-retained placenta

5. Prolonged standing during shipping

6. Excessive water intake after exercise

7. Fat, unfit horses

8. Concussion from hard surfaces

Symptoms:

1. Bounding pulse in the digital arteries located behind the fetlock

2. Rise in pulse and respiratory rates, increased temperature of hoof and coronet, pain in hoof when pressure applied, especially in the toe area.

3. Front feet affected, but can be all four. The horse will stand "parked out" if it's just the front feet and will be "camped under" or have a normal stance if all four feet are involved.

4. Prone position for long periods, reluctant to stand.

Treatment:

1. Eliminate the causes, if possible.

2. Mineral oil can be given in the case of dietary cause.

3. Call your veterinarian.

4. Provide a light diet of leafy grass hay, only in small amounts initially.

5. Apply cold water to the legs, 3-4 times a day, 1/2 hour at a time.

Prevention:

1. Mare: treat retained placenta

2. Never over-feed and make diet changes slowly.

3. Take fat horses and ponies off rich fields.

4. Provide small amounts of water after a hard ride.

5. Condition horses before taking them out on hard rides or trips.

6. Avoid long, non-stop trailering; stop and exercise horses regularly.

- **WOUNDS/BLEEDING:** Here is a list of supplies to help you in case of a wound. These can be found in a drugstore or livestock supply store:

1. Antiseptic-Betadine

2. Surgical gauze roll

3. 1 lb. cotton roll

4. Gauze bandages, 6-4x4s

5. 4 oz. Sulfonamide or Furazolidone/Nitrofurazone

6. Large animal thermometer

7. Vet wrap and similar product

Type 1) Venous: Oozes or flows

Treatment (Venous): Direct pressure usually will control bleeding. Place a wad of gauze-covered cotton directly over wound and bandage over the top. If bleeding continues, apply more layers of bandage over previous layers until under control. Don't remove the previous layers! Penicillin can be given to the horse in the muscle: 20cc twice a day for 5 days. Avoid using Penicillin if there is an allergy. Betadine ointment can be applied to the wound then bandaged. Keep your horse up to date on tetanus vaccinations.

Type 2) Arterial: Spurts out

Treatment (Arterial): Apply direct pressure to wound and bandage as described for venous bleeding. To apply a tourniquet, place gauze above the wound over the arteries course; tighten it with a bandage to stop the bleeding. Never leave this on more than 15 minutes at a time because doing so cuts off the blood supply to all parts below the tourniquet. Release for 1 minute; then move it up or down from the previous area and repeat. Apply pressure to artery above the bleeding, if possible. If the bleeding cannot be controlled using direct pressure and pressure-point on the artery, then a tourniquet can be used on the extremities. After the bleeding has stopped completely, the wound can be washed and flushed with clean water and bandaged. Wounds over joints and tendons should be seen as soon as possible by your veterinarian to evaluate possible involvement into the joint or tendon structures.

- **OCULAR (EYE) EMERGENCIES:** An ocular injury on the trail can cause a puncture, cut, bruise or an abrasion of the eye.

Treatment:

1. Bruise, use a cold compress

2. Abrasion/laceration - call your veterinarian.

3. Antibiotic ointment can be helpful. If a foreign body is in the eye, wash it with saline or water (no soap).

Prognosis: A puncture or scratch on the corneal surface may result in corneal opacity - clouding of the eye. The quicker the treatment, the better the chance of recovery. Horses have very strong eyelid muscles, and it can be very difficult to examine and treat the eye. It is usually best to have the eye thoroughly examined by a veterinarian. Lacerations or punctures through the corner or sclera (white part) into the inner structure of the eye are emergency situations which demand immediate veterinary care to save the eye and sight.

Other Emergencies

- **LOST SHOE:** Easyboots have saved many hooves in the hills. Be sure to carry the correct size for your stock. Using a leather strap around the inside heel helps to get the boot on. (Remove the strap after placement.)

- **TACK BREAKS:** Carry a bag of sturdy, various length and width of leather pieces. Sometimes one part of the saddle can be used in a totally different way.

- **WASPS/BEES:** Nests are found hanging in trees, in old rotting stumps and in the ground. Usually the first several riders stir things up a bit and the rest of the group get the brunt of the situation. The stock will probably run forward quickly, striking out and possibly start bucking. They stomp to remove the stinging pests. (Luckily, you are usually in the trees when this happens.) Just move forward, out of the area as quickly as possible and hope your mount doesn't panic.

- **KEYS:** Always leave keys at the rig and make sure someone knows the location of the keys and your riding destination. In an emergency, anyone should be able to use each rig.

Pete Lake

Trail Notes:

_____

_____

_____

_____

_____

_____

_____

_____

_____

_____

Ranger District Information

Washington

Chelan Ranger District 428 W. Woodin Ave. Chelan, WA 98816 (509) 682-2576 or (509) 664-2702	Cle Elum Ranger District 803 W. 2nd Cle Elum, WA 98922 (509) 674-4411
Entiat Ranger District P.O. Box 476 Entiat, WA 98822 (509) 784-1511	Lake Wenatchee Ranger District 22976 Hwy. 207 Leavenworth, WA 98826 (509) 763-3103 or (509) 664-2704
Leavenworth Ranger District 600 Sherbourne Leavenworth, WA 98826 (509) 548-6977	Marblemount Ranger District 2105 Star Route 20 Sedro Wooley, WA 98284 (509) 873-4590
Methow Ranger District P.O. Box 188 Twisp, WA 98856 (509) 977-2131	Naches Ranger District 510 Hwy. 12 Naches, WA 98937 (509) 653-2205 or (509) 664-2719
Okanogan Ranger District 1240 S. 2nd Okanogan, WA 98840 (509) 826-3275	Tonasket Ranger District #1 West Winesap Tonasket, WA 98855 (509) 486-2186
Winthrop Ranger District P.O. Box 579 Winthrop, WA 98826 (509) 996-2266	Alpine Lakes Wilderness Hotline (800) 627-0062 - toll free (206) 775-9702 - Seattle

Oregon

Bear Valley Ranger District 528 Main St. John Day, OR 97845 (541) 575-2110	Bend Ranger District 1230 NE 3rd Suite, A262 Bend, OR 97701 (541) 388-5664
Deschutes National Forest 1645 Hwy. 20 E. Bend, OR 97701 (541) 388-2715	Detroit Ranger District HC 73, Box 320 Mill City, OR 97360 (541) 854-3366
Malheur National Forest 139 N.E. Daytona John Day, OR 97845 (541) 575-1731	Mt. Hood National Forest 2955 N.W. Division St. Gresham, OR 97030 (503) 666-0700
Mt. Hood Visitor Center 65000 E. Hwy. 26 Welches, OR 97067 (503) 622-5741	Ochoco National Forest 155 N. Court St. Prineville, OR 97754 (541) 447-6247
Prineville Ranger District 3160 N.E. 3rd, P.O. Box 490 Prineville, OR 97754 (541) 447-6247	Wallowa Valley Ranger District 88401 Hwy. 82 Enterprise, OR 97828 (541) 426-4978
Wallowa-Whitman National Forest 1550 Dewey Ave. Baker, OR 97814 (541) 523-6391	Willamette National Forest 211 East 7th P.O. Box 10607 Eugene, OR 97440 (541) 465-6522

Internet (WWW) Addresses

Current road and trail info:	http://www.fs.fed.us/
Alpine Lakes Homepage:	http://www.washington.edu/trails/alpine
Other pages of interest:	http://www.wta.org/wta http://www.nature.org http://empnet/dnf/desnf/dnfhome.html http://www.dirtnw.com//wwwboard/messages1/42.html http://www.proaxis.com/~percyb/ http://www.eburg.com/~rusho>

Saddlebag Snacks

Dehydrated cranberry leather: Take several cans of jellied cranberry sauce, slice into one-quarter-inch rounds, lay on oiled trays and dry for 12-24 hours, depending on how leathery you like them. Store in Ziplock bags in the refrigerator.

Bagel sandwiches: Bagels are a sturdy choice for saddlebag lunches. Our favorite is an onion bagel, cream cheese, alfalfa sprouts, and sliced cucumber with a dash of pepper. Another is an onion bagel, cream cheese, ham and sprouts. Roll these up in plastic wrap and they'll survive just about anything!

Canned meat or fish: Tuna, sardines, vienna sausages or deviled ham with crackers are quick and easy and have lots of protein.

Old standby snacks: Carrots, jerky, trail mix, cheese, apples and an assortment of hard and chewy bulk candy are easy to carry. Pack out all candy wrappers!

Freeze your juice and water at least the night before. This helps keep your lunch nice and cool and boy, does it taste good on those sizzling afternoons. A slice of lemon in your water is very refreshing.

*Josie on
Bagby Trail*

ALWAYS bring more food than you need in case of an emergency.

Foil:
- Dishpan: Dig hole and line with foil

- Cup: Mold around the bottom of can

- Strainer: Form bowl and prick holes in the bottom

- Scour pad: Wad up foil and start cleaning.

- Foil has to be packed out

The more you prepare at home, the more you can enjoy the campfire, family and friends. Cut up vegetables and store in Ziplock bags. Marinate meat in bags. We all work up a mountain of an appetite when we're outdoors.

Pack out all foil, cans and uneaten food. Contain food from bears by using bear resistant panniers or making a food hoist. Always leave camp cleaner than you found it.

Pam, Rene & Josie
along Ingalls Creek

Camp Food

Beef 'n stuff: Brown hamburger, add chopped onions, potatoes and carrots. When vegetables are tender, add cream of mushroom soup and Worcestershire sauce. Serve over cooked noodles. Another way is to brown the burger and onions, add catsup and BBQ sauce, and serve on buns.

Beef 'n Beans: Brown burger and onion. Add canned tomatoes, beans and BBQ sauce. (It's good with corn bread.)

Fish: If you've been lucky and have caught some fish, dip them in an egg-beer mixture. Roll in cracker crumbs and fry till golden brown on each side. Another way is to cut into fillets with skin on and sprinkle with seasoning salt. Grill covered, with skin side down, on greased rack 5 inches above the coals for about 15 minutes and baste with butter and garlic. (Done when flaky.)

Liver and onions: Slice liver thin. Coat with flour, salt, pepper, and parsley. Brown lightly on each side and remove from pan. Add onions to the pan and saute. Add some of the flour mixture to the pan and add milk. Stir till bubbly and smooth. Add liver and simmer 25 minutes.

Grouse: (When in season and hunting has been good.) Rub the grouse breasts with oil and grill over coals with salt and pepper. Coal-baked potatoes and canned corn make a great meal.

Flapjacks: Oil up the grill, mix the batter and throw in all those huckleberries!

Goulash: Brown hamburger and onion, add garlic and chili powder, and stir in canned tomatoes and beans. Add equal amounts of water and rice, and add chopped green pepper. Cover and simmer 25 minutes. Dish up and serve with grated cheese and tortilla chips.

Grilled tuna sandwich: Just that!

BBQ meats: Cut up your choice of hot dogs, German sausages or Little Smokies. Put in a skillet with BBQ sauce, and heat through. It makes a good warm snack.

Chili: Brown burger and onions; add canned tomatoes and beans and spices. Top with cheese.

Rene's Rolls: Mix together: Sliced hot dogs, cubed cheese, chopped onion, chopped boiled eggs, chili sauce and mayonnaise. Fill hamburger buns with mixture, wrap in foil and place over fire for 30 minutes. (These freeze well.)

Ogan Boys' Beef Heroes: Fry up bacon; remove and brown hamburger and onion. Add olives, catsup, salt, pepper and chili powder. Cook 5 minutes; place slice of bacon, colby cheese, meat mixture, and a slice of muenster cheese on bun. Wrap in foil and place over coals 20 minutes.

Easy Camp Soup: Cook elbow macaroni. Brown burger and add pepper, oregano, basil, salt, 1 pkg. onion soup mix, 3 C. water, 8 oz. tomato sauce and 1 tbsp. soy sauce. Add any vegetables you like and cook till done. Add macaroni and serve with parmesan cheese.

On the Grill: Old BBQ grills from home work great while camping (you pack it in - you pack it out!)

Josie's Grilled Cheese: Place cheese inside pita bread and oil the outside. Wrap in foil and place on grill. (Tomatoes and onions added are good.)

Burrito: Put a filling of beans, rice, cheese, beef or whatever you like in the tortilla; oil; wrap in foil; and grill. Add tomatoes and salsa when done. Dig in!

K-Bobs: Make early and marinate. Use beef, chicken or prawns. Put a large mushroom on the skewer first to hold on the food; then alternate with peppers, onions and tomatoes. Use BBQ or teriyaki sauce. (Snyder's sauce is great.) Grill evenly and enjoy.

German or Hot Beer Sausage: Roast on a stick; smother in sauerkraut and mustard on a bun - Yum!

Ellensburg Local Road Rides

(See map following)

1. Coleman Canyon
2. Cooke Canyon
3. Green Canyon
4. Lillard Hill
5. Naneum Canyon
6. North Fork Manastash
7. Robinson Canyon
8. Schnebly Canyon
9. Stone Quarry
10. Joe Watt Canyon
11. Umptanum

Josie in Green Canyon

- **Coleman Canyon:** Nice ride along the creek. Fairly flat, then climbs after 3 miles.

- **Cooke Canyon:** Level road ride along a creek. Access to powerline road. Cattle trails along the side of the road.

- **Green Canyon:** Begins flat and steepens quickly.

- **Lillard Hill:** Begins climbing on an open hillside, then into forest. Good valley views.

- **Naneum Canyon:** Pleasant road ride with a creek along side. Cattle trails in bottom of canyon with lots of wire down.

- **North Fork Manastash:** Nice, forested road ride with some easy climbs. Parking on the north side of the road, near the wooden sign. (Closed in elk-feeding season.)

- **Robinson Canyon:** Good road ride through the forest. Some climbing. Spring brings out the rattlesnakes. (Closed during elk feeding.)

- **Schnebly Canyon:** This is in sagebrush and forest. Old logging roads available for loops. Some cattle trails and old wire fencing.

- **Stone Quarry:** Great views once you reach the upper section. Target practicers and motorcyclists frequent this spot.

- **Joe Watt Canyon:** Good ride with excellent game trails to follow everywhere. Perfect for cross country roaming. Watch for fence lines. (Closed during elk feeding.)

- **Umptanum:** Long loop rides on open roads with good panoramic views.

Use common sense and close all gates. Leave your dogs at home and spread manure away from parking areas. Ranchers pay for the use of some of this range land. Respect all private property. Loops are possible in all of these areas. Have fun exploring.

ELLENSBURG LOCAL MAP

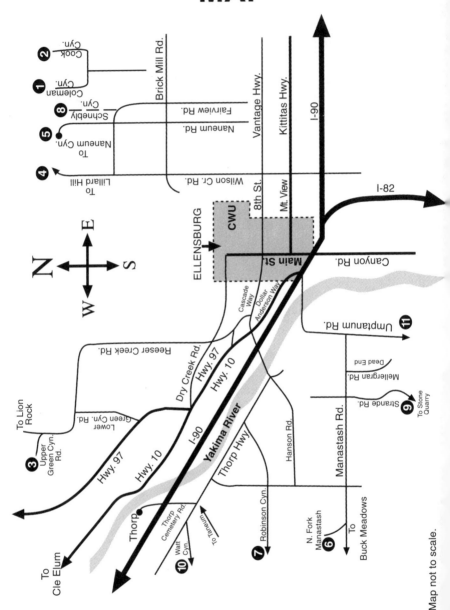

Map not to scale.

Salmon La Sac

Salmon La Sac area has so much to offer. It's easily accessed, has an established horse camp, well-maintained trails and oodles of loop possibilities. Black bear are common in this area. The trails vary from steep ridgetops to gentle, wide paths. The berry picking in the fall is out of this world. Most trails are in wilderness boundaries, so there are no motorcyclists. If you're planning a trip here, you might want to plan in the middle of the week. (It can be a very busy place.) As always, read and obey all wilderness rules. Remember to store food in bear-proof panniers or use a food hoist. Keep stock at least 200 ft. from all water sources.

Salmon La Sac Index	Trail #
Cooper River	1311
Deception Pass Loop to	1371, 1059, 1059A,
Cathedral Rock	2000, 1345
Deep Lake	1396.1
Escondido Lake	1320
Jolly Mountain	1307
Jolly Mountain Spur	1307.1
Kachess Ridge	1315
Lake Michael	1336
Pacific Crest Trail	2000
(Spinola Creek to Deep Lake)	
Paddy-Go-Easy Pass	1595.1
Paris Creek	1393.1
Pete Lake	1323
Pollalie Ridge	1309
Sasse Mountain	1340
Spinola Creek	1310.1
Tired Creek	1317
Trail Creek	1322
Waptus Pass	1329
Waptus River	1310

SALMON LA SAC

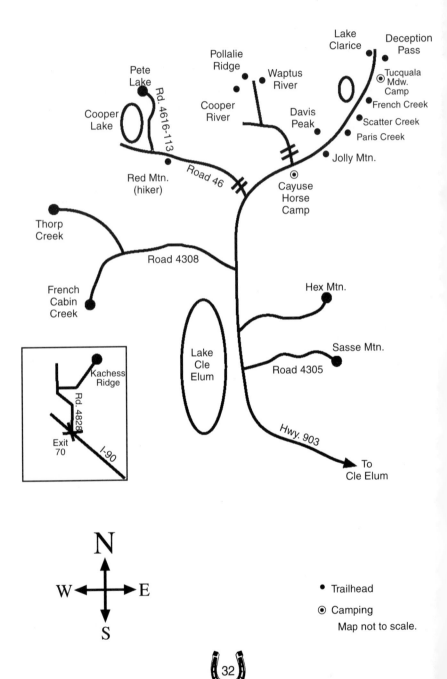

Lake Clarice
Deception Pass
Pollalie Ridge
Waptus River
Pete Lake
Tucquala Mdw. Camp
Rd. 4616-113
Cooper River
French Creek
Cooper Lake
Davis Peak
Scatter Creek
Paris Creek
Road 46
Jolly Mtn.
Red Mtn. (hiker)
Cayuse Horse Camp
Thorp Creek
Road 4308
French Cabin Creek
Hex Mtn.
Lake Cle Elum
Sasse Mtn.
Road 4305
Kachess Ridge
Rd. 4828
Exit 70
I-90
Hwy. 903
To Cle Elum

N
W ← → E
S

• Trailhead
◉ Camping
Map not to scale.

32

Cooper River #1311

Length:	3.9 miles
Elevation:	2500'-2800'
Map:	GTM 208 Kachess Lake
Rating:	Easy

Trailhead Directions: Take Highway 903 north from Cle Elum to Salmon La Sac. Pass the Cayuse Horse Camp and cross the bridge. Stay to the right on the dirt road. The trailhead is .5 mile further. A large drive-through loop makes for easy access with tie rails, ramp and outhouses. Cooper River Trail is one-quarter mile from the parking area and is the furthest trail to the left.

Other Trails Accessed: 1310, 1309, 1323

Camping: Cayuse Horse Camp has corrals, a horse ramp, tables, several drive-through sites, water and is a fee-charged camp. Outhouses and fire pits are available.

Trail: The Cooper River Trail starts at the Salmon La Sac Trailhead at 2400' and travels west, then north. It follows Cooper River and is beautiful as it travels through dense forest. There are lots of berries to pick. Black bear have been seen on this trail numerous times. The trail has small inclines and declines and ends when you reach Road 4616. To continue to Pete Lake Trailhead, ride the road (approximately 1 mile) and stay to the right until you reach the trailhead.

Deception Pass Loop to Cathedral Rock #1376
(Trails: 2000, 1059, 1059A, 1345)

Length:	23 miles
Elevation:	3400'-5600'
Map:	GTM 176 Stevens Pass
Rating:	Easy-Medium (length)

Trailhead Directions: From Cle Elum, take Highway 903 north to Salmon La Sac. Stay right on Fish Lake Road 4330 until the road ends.

Other Trails Accessed: 1066, 1322

Trail: Deception Pass Trail #1376 heads north five miles, winding through meadows and along Hyas Lake. You'll climb the mountainside in forest, passing some swampy areas to join the PCT #2000. On this loop ride, stay right on the PCT #2000 and ride north through forest (with one short narrow spot), then open hillsides. At 3.5 miles, spur Trail #1059A descends left. Either take this now or ride on to Deception Lakes, which is one-quarter mile up the trail for a nice lunch spot. The spur trail is only .8 mile and winds you down to Deception Creek Trail #1059. Head south, left, on Deception Creek Trail and travel 3 miles through meadows, forest and several creek crossings back up to Deception Pass. Now head south on the PCT #2000 for 5 miles, riding below Mount Daniels Glacier and Cathedral Rock. High waters in early season may hinder your travels. At Cathedral Pass, take Cathedral Rock Trail #1345 to the left for the last 4.5 miles. Switchback down past Squaw Lake, staying left on Trail #1345 back to the truck. Excellent scenery in the fall, especially on the PCT portions.

Deep Lake #1396.1

Length:	.5 miles
Elevation:	4400'
Map:	GTM 176 Stevens Pass
Rating:	Easy

Trailhead Directions: No trailhead

Other Trails Accessed: PCT 2000

Trail: Deep Lake Trail #1396.1 is a short section, taking you into Deep Lake, which is set in a bowl. The dark blue color lets us know how deep it really is. Please preserve the vegetation around the lake

Escondido Lake #1320

Length:	1.8 miles
Elevation:	4100'-4600'
Map:	GTM 208 Kachess Lake
Rating:	Medium

Trailhead Directions: No trailhead

Other Trails Accessed: 1329

Trail: Escondido Trail heads northwest from Waptus Pass Trail. It runs along side Escondido Creek, climbing steeply in a few sections. There is a good sized meadow at the lake.

Jolly Mountain #1307

Length:	6.2 miles
Elevation:	2400'-6443'
Map:	GTM 208 Kachess Lake
Rating:	Medium (climbing)

Trailhead Directions: Drive Highway 903 north from Cle Elum to Cayuse Horse Camp at Salmon La Sac. The trailhead is at the far end of the campground, near the corrals with day parking available.

Other Trails Accessed: 1307.1, 1222, 1353, 1340, 1355

Camping: Cayuse Horse Camp has some drive-through sites, picnic tables, fire pits, group sites, water, outhouses, horse ramp, corrals, and day parking. A fee is charged.

Trail: Jolly Mountain Trail #1307 starts at 2400' and climbs for 3 miles going through old clear-cuts and forest, switchbacking most of the time. At 3.2 miles, 4700', the trail turns south at the intersection with Jolly Mountain Spur Trail #1307.1. Next you'll climb to 5600' for 1 mile to join Sasse Ridge Trail #1340. You'll pass the West Fork Teanaway Trail and climb up Jolly Mountain to 6443', where the trail ends. Yellow Hill Trail #1222 continues from here.

Jolly Mountain Spur #1307.1

Length:	2.1 miles
Elevation:	4200'-5200'
Map:	GTM 208 Kachess Lake
Rating:	Medium-Hard (steep)

Trailhead Directions: No trailhead

Other Trails Accessed: 1307, 1393.1

Trail: Jolly Mountain Spur Trail is 2.1 miles and connects Paris Creek Trail to Jolly Mountain Trail. It climbs to 5200' and drops back to meet Paris Creek Trail at 4200'. The trail is in good shape, forested the whole way and has steep inclines and declines.

Kachess Ridge #1315

Length:	14.5 miles
Elevation:	2400'-5300'
Map:	GTM 208 Kachess Lake
Rating:	Medium-Hard (narrow)

Trailhead Directions: Take exit 70 from I-90, go left on the north side of I-90 to Forest Service Road 4818. Drive .5 mile past the powerlines and take the road to the right, which ends .3 miles from the trailhead. A small parking area is available.

Other Trails Accessed: 1308.1, 1305, 1315.1, 1316, 1330

Trail: Kachess Ridge Trail #1315 starts climbing immediately through forest, crossing Silver Creek several times. You'll pass through a meadow, then a quick, steep drop puts you in French Creek Basin. Climb out through an old clear-cut and follow the ridges crossing sidehills. Drop into Thorp Lake for lunch, or climb to the lookout. Continue north past the lookout, riding mostly through forest, across No Name Ridge to a spur road, above Cooper Pass. This is the end of the trail. (The last 5.5 miles tend to have logs down, and is seldom used.)

This is a great scenic ride. I've sighted mountain goats numerous times on the steep, rocky hillsides. There are several difficult spots on the trail, such as rock out-croppings, steep open cliffs and the trail seems to be inclining or declining steeply most of the time. One of my favorite rides!

Rene

Lake Michael #1336

Length:	6 miles
Elevation:	4300'-5700'
Map:	GTM 208 Kachess Lake
Rating:	Medium

Trailhead Directions: No trailhead

Other Trails Accessed: 1322

Trail: Lake Michael ascends from Trail Creek Trail #1322 at 4300'. It heads southeast and has no trails branching off of it. You'll switchback up across a rocky hillside, bringing you to a split in the trail. Left takes you around Lake Michael; right continues 2 miles more to Lake Terence. Lake Michael is nestled in a bowl, which has yellow-bellied marmots and plenty of wildflowers. The elevation is 5100' at the lake. The trail is in good shape and has good footing. Continuing right across the outlet stream, the trail to Lake Terence climbs up the west side of Lake Michael. Travel through small meadow areas with occasional views of Mount Rainier. Please keep stock 200' from the lakes.

Pacific Crest Trail #2000

(Spinola Creek to Deep Lake)

Length:	3.5 miles
Elevation:	3400'-4400'
Map:	GTM 176 Stevens Pass
Rating:	Medium (climbing)

Trailhead Directions: No trailhead

Other Trails Accessed: 1310.1, 1365, 1396.1

Trail: This section of the PCT will take you from Waptus Lake area to Deep Lake Trail #1396.1. It starts from Spinola Creek Trail #1310.1 and heads north along the west side of Spinola Creek. When you ride here, you feel you're "in the woods." It is very revitalizing. There are some open sidehills towards the top; they're short and the trail is good. The trail levels off as it nears the intersection with Lake Vicente Trail #1365 and .5 mile further is the Deep Lake Trail cutoff.

Paddy-Go-Easy Pass #1595.1

Length:	3 miles
Elevation:	3400'-6100'
Map:	GTM 176 Stevens Pass
Rating:	Medium

Trailhead Directions: Take Highway 903 out of Cle Elum to Salmon La Sac and take Fish Lake Road 4330, 11.5 miles. Just past Fish Lake Guard Station the trailhead is on the right with a very small parking area.

Other Trails Accessed: 1559

Trail: Paddy-Go-Easy Pass Trail begins by crossing a creek, then start a short, steep climb for 3 miles. Ride through forest, crossing several creeks, and some challenging spots, such as jumping around roots and rocks. Cross small grassy hillsides and ride beneath the 6500' rocky cliff, then crest Paddy-Go-Easy Pass with Sprite Lake near! This is a short and quick way to enjoy the views of surrounding mountains. A moderate challenge for stock and rider.

Paris Creek #1393.1

Length:	8 miles
Elevation:	2800'-4200'
Map:	GTM 208 Kachess Lake
Rating:	Medium

Trailhead Directions: Take Highway 903 out of Cle Elum to Salmon La Sac, go past the Cayuse Horse Camp and take the dirt Forest Service Road 4330 to the right. It is 2 miles to the trailhead. Paris Creek Trail and Davis Peak Trail share the same trailhead. Paris Creek is on the right side of the road.

Other Trails Accessed: 1307.1, 1392.1, 1393, 1392.7

Trail: Paris Creek Trail #1393.1 starts at 2800' in open forest and black bear have been spotted here. The trail climbs east through the forest in and out of a clear-cut with Paris Creek as your companion. You'll come to the intersection with Trail #1307.1 at 4200'. From there, you'll climb steeply out of the basin, then down to join the Middle Fork Teanaway Trail #1393, where Paris Creek Trail ends. Some sections are steep and narrow. (Loop possibility with Trail #1307.1.)

Pete Lake #1323

Length:	7.5 miles
Elevation:	2800'-3200'
Map:	GTM 207 Snoqualmie Pass GTM 208 Kachess Lake
Rating:	Easy

Trailhead Directions: Take Highway 903 from Cle Elum, turn left across the bridge on Road 46. Follow the signs to Road 4616-113 to the Pete Lake Trailhead. There is a large parking area with an outhouse.

Other Trails Accessed: 1311, 1317, 1329, 1323.2, 1323.3, 2000, 1323.1, 1323.4

Trail: Pete Lake Trail #1323 starts at the far end of Cooper Lake. The trail is flat, wandering through forest. At 1.4 miles, Tired Creek Trail #1317 heads north. You'll cross numerous small creeks. At 2.6 miles, intersect Road Tie Trail #1323.1. Pete Lake is a nice spot to enjoy. The trail winds around the northwest end of the lake. Waptus Pass Trail #1329 exits from the trail; then Lemah Meadow Trail #1323.2, heads to the right. Stay left and cross Lemah Creek; then climb through forest to join Sheep Camp Trail

Pete Lake

#1323.3. In one-quarter mile further, you'll join the PCT #2000, where the trail ends. The majority of the trail is wide and has an easy grade with several climbing areas.

Get Pugsley

One summer, a friend and I were trying out a new horse named Champ. We were headed into Pete Lake from Salmon La Sac. We'd only ridden a mile past Cooper Lake and came upon a man with a backpack, who looked tired, worried and was swimming in sweat. He said his son had sprained his ankle and he was going back to Cooper Lake to drop off his pack and then returning to get his son. We offered our help, and rode till we came upon a very large, 12-year-old boy who looked like Pugsley on The Adams Family Show! We knew one gelding rode double, so we hoisted Pugsley up; then I put on his pack, got on Champ, and gently eased our way down the trail. Pugsley's pack was 3' high and weighed 40 lbs.! Wow! It was top-heavy. I put Champ's nose in the other gelding's tail and we ventured out. It was quite challenging crossing the creeks! We made it! The father was relieved and so were we! Champ was really a champ that day!

Josie

Pollalie Ridge #1309

Length:	8.8 miles
Elevation:	2500'-5500'
Map:	GTM 208 Kachess Lake
Rating:	Medium-Hard (climbing)

Trailhead Directions: Drive Highway 903 from Cle Elum to Salmon La Sac, past the Cayuse Horse Camp, cross the bridge and stay right on the dirt road to the trailhead. A large loop turn around is available for easy parking. Tie rails, ramps and outhouses are provided. Pollalie Ridge Trail is the center trail one-quarter mile from the parking area.

Other Trails Accessed: 1311, 1310, 1329, 1317

Camping: Cayuse Horse Camp has some drive-through camp spots, outhouse, fire pits, corrals, water, and tables. It is a fee-charged camp. Day parking is available.

Trail: Pollalie Ridge Trail #1309 follows the ridge and travels northwest. There are many elevation changes with a steady incline the first 3 miles. Diamond Lake is at the 4-mile point at 4800'. You'll ride through meadows, forest and across the ridgetops with breathtaking views, especially at the old look-out. The glaciers to the west and north are awesome. Travel 1 mile down to connect with Tired Creek Trail #1317, which drops to the west. Nice switchbacks take you down through old forest to Waptus Pass at 4200'.

We usually ride the Pollalie Ridge Trail beginning at the north end at Waptus Pass, your stock will agree with this decision. The steady climb at the south end isn't our idea of a nice, slow warm-up for their legs! The trail is in good shape.

Rene on Pollalie Ridge

Sasse Mountain #1340

Length:	9 miles
Elevation:	3600'-5700'
Map:	GTM 208 Kachess Lake
Rating:	Medium-Hard (narrow)

Trailhead Directions: Drive Highway 903 from Cle Elum and take a right on Forest Service Road 4305, which is just past the Last Resort Restaurant. Drive Road 4305 to Road 118. There is a small parking area with no facilities.

Other Trails Accessed: 1343, 1307, 1340.1

Trail: Sasse Mountain Trail is described from the south. It climbs steadily to Hex Mountain at 5300'. The trail is somewhat rough in places from heavy use. You'll follow ridgetops with excellent views of the surrounding mountains. Prepare for lots of climbing, sidehills and several rock outcroppings. This trail hasn't been updated and is fairly rugged. The section between Hex Mountain and Little Salmon La Sac Trail is closed to motorized use. Along the ridgetops, you'll encounter rocky and grassy hillsides, logging activity, lush forest and good views of Lake Cle Elum. No loops possible. Possible point to point with 2 rigs. **Recommended for experienced teams only!**

Spinola Creek #1310.1

Length:	.9 miles
Elevation:	3100'-3400'
Map:	GTM 176 Stevens Pass
Rating:	Medium

Trailhead Directions: No trailhead

Other Trails Accessed: 1310, 2000

Trail: Spinola Creek Trail is only .9 mile long and runs between the Waptus Horse Ford, #1329.1, and the hiker foot bridge #1310 to the PCT #2000. It heads north along the west side of Spinola Creek.

Greg Up Tired Creek

Tired Creek #1317

Length:	3.8 miles
Elevation:	2900'-5400'
Map:	GTM 208 Kachess Lake
Rating:	Medium

Trailhead Directions: No trailhead.

Other Trails Accessed: 1323, 1309

Trail: Tired Creek Trail leaves the Pete Lake Trail at 1.5 miles. The trail is in good condition all the way, with a moderate, steady climb and excellent views in the upper portions. The lower section goes through a select-cut logging area. (When the trail joins a road, go right one hundred yards to gain trail access again.) The trail heads left off the road to climb rapidly along Tired Creek. Ride through forest on switchbacks and into the open upper bowls of Tired Creek and Alpine Wilderness. The trail ends where it joins Pollalie Ridge Trail.

Trail Creek #1322

Length:	5.5 miles
Elevation:	2900'-4400'
Map:	GTM 176 Stevens Pass
	GTM 208 Kachess Lake
Rating:	Medium (climbing)

Trailhead Directions: No trailhead

Other Trails Accessed: 1310, 1336, 1345

Trail: Trail Creek Trail #1322 goes northeast from Waptus River Trail #1310. It starts at the river, then switches up and levels out several times. Following Trail Creek, you'll hear and catch a glimpse of a waterfall. At 2.5 miles, Lake Michael Trail joins from the right. The last 2.8 miles of trail continues at a much gentler grade. The whole trail is in forest and as we were, you may be glad on a 90+ degree day! The trail ends as it connects with Cathedral Rock Trail #1345 at 4400'.

Waptus Pass #1329

Length:	6 miles
Elevation:	3000'-4200'
Map:	GTM 208 Kachess Lake
Rating:	Medium

Trailhead Directions: No trailhead

Other Trails Accessed: 1323, 1320, 1329.3, 1309, 1310

Trail: Waptus Pass Trail #1329 exits the Pete Lake Trail at 4.4 miles and switchbacks for close to 1 mile in a northeasterly direction. You'll join Escondido Lake Trail #1320 at 1.7 miles. In .7 mile more, the Waptus Burn Trail #1329.3 connects from the north. Then Pollalie Ridge Trail exits to the south. Wind along a plateau section; then switchback down to join the Waptus Lake Trail #1310. This trail allows you to ride a great loop, incorporating Pete Lake and Waptus River Trails

Waptus River #1310

Length:	11.2 miles
Elevation:	2500'-3100'
Map:	GTM 208 Kachess Lake
	GTM 176 Stevens Pass
Rating:	Easy

Trailhead Directions: Drive Highway 903 from Cle Elum to Salmon La Sac, past the Cayuse Horse Camp. Cross the bridge and stay to the right on the dirt road for .5 miles to the trailhead. There are tie rails, ramp, outhouses and a loop drive that makes for easy access. Waptus River Trail is the far right trail one-quarter mile from parking.

Other Trails Accessed: 1311, 1322, 1329, 1310.1, 1337, 2000

Camping: Cayuse Horse Camp has corrals, some drive-through spots, outhouses, fire pits, tables, and water. It is a fee-charged camp. Day parking available.

Waptus Lake

50

Trail: Waptus River Trail shares the same trailhead as Cooper River Trail, far left, and Pollalie Ridge Trail, center. Waptus River Trail is the far right trail that mostly rolls along the entire 11.2 miles. You'll parallel the river and enjoy the rock formations as this wide trail with good footing travels through forest, past ponds full of lily pads and at 7.3 miles junctions Trail Creek Trail #1322. Waptus Pass Trail exits in 2 miles more. The hiker foot bridge trail stays to the right; the horse ford is one-quarter mile further on Trail #1329.1. Waptus River Trail winds around the east then, north rim of Waptus Lake as Spade Lake Trail #1337 joins from the north. The trail ends 1.3 miles further as it joins the PCT #2000.

Taneum and Manastash Areas

The Taneum and Manastash areas were the first trails we explored after arriving in the wondrous Kittitas Valley. These areas provide you with excellent opportunities to get snapshots of Mount Rainier and the Stuart Range. There are small lakes and streams and the trees are somewhat thinner than they are in the Salmon La Sac area. This gives a more open feeling. There are big meadows to lunch in and many loops to explore. We share this area with motorcyclists, hik-

Quartz Mtn.
Outhouse

ers and mountain bikers, so give them respect and we're sure you'll get the same in return. In fact, when the Forest Service hasn't cleared the trails, the horse people and others join up to work together on clearing logs. If you see initials on the cut logs, they may have been sawed by someone you now know! Taneum Forest Service Road 33 is paved.

Trot On...

Taneum-Manastash Index	Trail #
Blaze Ridge	1333
Cle Elum Ridge	1326
Fishhook Flat	1378
Frost Mountain	1366
Gooseberry Flat	1227
Granite Creek	1326.1
Greek Creek	1321.2
Keenan Meadow	1386
Lightning Point	1377.1

Little Creek Basin	1334
Manastash Lake	1350
Manastash Ridge	1388
(Quartz Mountain to Mount Clifty)	
Mount Clifty	1321.1
North Fork Taneum	1377
North Ridge	1321
Shoestring lake	1385
South Fork Taneum	1367
Taneum Ridge	1363

Trail Notes

_____

_____

_____

_____

_____

_____

_____

_____

_____

_____

_____

_____

_____

TANEUM AND MANASTASH

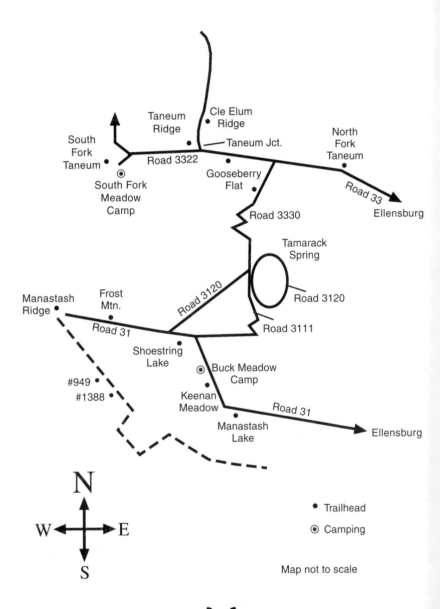

Taneum Ridge

Cle Elum Ridge

Taneum Jct.

North Fork Taneum

South Fork Taneum

Road 3322

Gooseberry Flat

South Fork Meadow Camp

Road 33

Ellensburg

Road 3330

Tamarack Spring

Manastash Ridge

Frost Mtn.

Road 3120

Road 3120

Road 31

Road 3111

Shoestring Lake

Buck Meadow Camp

#949

#1388

Keenan Meadow

Road 31

Ellensburg

Manastash Lake

N
W   E
S

• Trailhead

◉ Camping

Map not to scale

54

BLAZED RIDGE

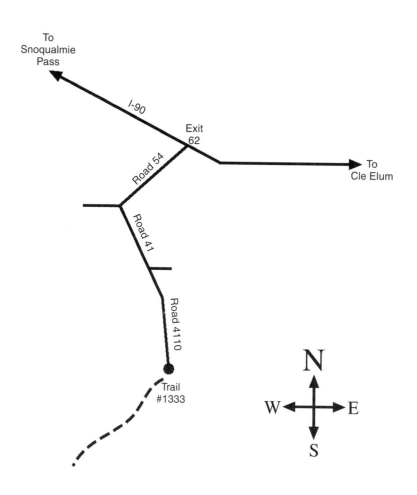

To
Snoqualmie
Pass

I-90

Exit
62

Road 54

To
Cle Elum

Road 41

Road 4110

Trail
#1333

N

W • E

S

• Trailhead

◉ Camping

Map not to scale

Blazed Ridge #1333

Length:	4.6 miles
Elevation:	4100'-5500'
Map:	GTM 240 Easton
Rating:	Easy-Medium (climbing)

Trailhead Directions: Take the Stampede Pass exit 62 off I-90. Drive southwest on Road 54, south on Road 41, south on 4110 crossing Big Creek, then climb to the trailhead. A small parking area is available.

Other Trails Accessed: 1341, 1321.2, 1388

Trail: Blazed Ridge Trail #1333 begins climbing through the forest, then continues on ridgetops to the end of the trail, where it joins with Manastash Ridge Trail #1388. You'll cross open ridges and sidehills with great views of the surrounding ridges. Mountain goats are seen frequently. We like making a loop using this trail starting at the North Ridge Trailhead, around Mount Clifty, out Blazed Ridge Trail, through Greek Creek Trail, then back down the North Ridge Trail. This trail is maintained and is seldom used. Use an updated GTM.

Cle Elum Ridge #1326

Length:	15.1 miles
Elevation:	2800-5800'
Map:	GTM 240 Easton GTM 241 Cle Elum
Rating:	Easy-Medium (climbing)

Trailhead Directions: No trailhead

Other Trails Accessed: 1377, 1377.1, 1326.1, 1334, 1321, 1388

Camping: Primitive camping at the Taneum Junction Trailhead with an outhouse and stream water for the stock. Bring potable water. We share this area with motorcyclists. No fee.

Trail: The Cle Elum Ridge Trail starts approximately 3 miles up the North Fork Taneum Trail from the Ice Water Campground or 1 mile up the North Fork Taneum Trail from the Taneum Junction. You'll follow the ridges inclining and declining numerous times. A portion has been rerouted and is signed. The trail junctions Granite Creek Trail at 8 miles, Little Creek Basin Trail at 9 miles, and Lightning Point Trail at 11 miles. The last climb has great views. Take long switchbacks down to Windy Pass at 5300' to connect with the North Fork Taneum Trail #1377. Trail #1326 heads south for approximately 1 mile, where the trail ends as it joins with Manastash Ridge Trail #1388. One day, as we approached Windy Pass, a herd of deer cautiously moved over for us. We tied up the horses, ate lunch and watched the deer graze nearby.

*Lightning Point Trail has been reassigned the number #1377.1.

Fishhook Flat #1378

Length:	4.2 miles
Elevation:	3600'-4200'
Map:	GTM 240 Easton
Rating:	Easy-Medium (climbing)

Trailhead Directions: No trailhead

Other Trails Accessed: 1377, 1367, 1363

Trail: Fishhook Flat Trail #1378 connects the North Fork Taneum and the South Fork Taneum Trails crossing the Taneum Ridge Trail. From the North Fork Taneum Trail climb up to a ridge; then drop down to cross a creek. You'll wind along Fishhook Meadow, then ride up to cross Road 3300. The trail intersects Taneum Ridge Trail #1363, then drops down to its end at the South Fork Taneum Trail. Overall this is a great trail with good footing and trotting areas!

Frost Mountain #1366

Length:	4 miles
Elevation:	3600'-5300'
Map:	GTM 240 Easton
Rating:	Medium

Trailhead Directions: Take exit 109 from I-90 to Ellensburg. Go north on Canyon Road to the Subway Restaurant, then left on Umptanum Road to Manastash Road. Go right on Manastash Road, driving to gravel Forest Service Road 31, then 11 miles more to Buck Meadows. Stay left past Buck Meadows to Forest Service Road 3100, drive 5 miles more to the trailhead.

Other Trails Accessed: 1366.1, 1367, 1385

Trail: Frost Mountain Trail starts with the first .5 mile traveling through clear-cuts with logging roads. You'll cross a meadow area and can wander up to the lookout or continue on a forested trail, which now descends into the South Fork of the Taneum. The upper portion of the trail on the Taneum side is fairly rocky with loose dirt. The further you descend, the better the trail gets. You'll cross several creeks on nice long switchbacks. This trail is used by motorcyclists and mountain bikers. The trail crosses Frost Mountain to the south and connects with Shoestring Lake Trail.

Shaggy Mane

Gooseberry Flat #1227

Length:	1.1 miles
Elevation:	2800'-3500'
Map:	GTM 241 Cle Elum
Rating:	Medium

Trailhead Directions: Drive west from Ellensburg, and take Thorp exit 101 from I-90. Drive south on Thorp Highway 1 mile and go right on Thorp Cemetery Road, continuing it becomes Forest Service Road 33. From Cle Elum, take exit 93, Elk Heights, from I-90. Drive the Thorp Prairie Road paralleling the highway on the north, approximately 3 miles. Turn right and cross over I-90, to Thorp Cemetery Road. Turn right and drive west on Thorp Cemetery Road to Forest Service Road 33. Drive 8 miles more to Taneum Junction. Go left across the bridge on Road 3322. Take a sharp left down the small hill to the parking area. This is the Taneum Junction parking area.

Other Trails Accessed: None

Trail: Gooseberry Flat Trail goes straight up to Gooseberry Flat through a clear-cut. The trail begins on the south side of Taneum Creek in the campground. This trail has been ridden without a saddle by Josie. What a challenge to stay on! (It is said there is an Indian Woman's grave alongside of the trail!)

Granite Creek #1326.1

Length:	2.5 miles
Elevation:	3600'-5200'
Map:	GTM 240 Easton
Rating:	Medium - Hard (rugged climbing)

Trailhead Directions: Take exit 78 off I-90 and drive south to the first intersection. Turn left across the canal, driving south to Forest Service Road 4517, go left on Road 117 and stay on Road 117 to the trailhead.

Other Trails Accessed: 1326

Trail: Granite Creek Trail #1326.1 has an elevation change of 2600' in 2.3 miles, so this means some climbing! You'll begin on the west side of Granite Creek, then cross it to switchback up an eroded and deeply rutted trail. Stock travel is difficult in spots. The trail is closed to motorcyclists and is rugged due to water runoff. The upper portion is in better shape than the lower. It ends at 5200' as it connects with Cle Elum Ridge Trail #1326.

Greek Creek #1321.2

Length:	3.2 miles
Elevation:	4300'-5400'
Map:	GTM 240 Easton
Rating:	Medium

Trailhead Directions: No trailhead.

Other Trails Accessed: 1333, 1321

Trail: Greek Creek Trail #1321.2 runs east and west to connect Blazed Ridge and North Ridge Trails. The trail drops down into Greek Creek from Blazed Ridge on a fairly steep grade. Cross the creek; then a gentler grade brings you up the east side with several nice level trotting spots to join the North Ridge Trail on an open ridge at approximately 4300'.

*This trail is not noted on the Green Trail Map. (Use this map for a general idea.)

Keenan Meadow #1386

Length:	3.1 miles
Elevation:	4200'-4800'
Map:	GTM 241 Cle Elum
Rating:	Easy

Trailhead Directions: Take exit 109 from I-90 to Ellensburg. Go north on Canyon Road to the Subway Restaurant, left on Umptanum Road to Manastash Road. Go right on Manastash Road, driving to gravel Forest Service Road 31, then 11 miles more to Buck Meadows. This is the trailhead.

Other Trails Accessed: 1385

Camping: Buck Meadows Campground has an outhouse, table, and stock water. There is no fee. Bring potable water. This campground is scheduled to be moved to the south .5 mile by 1998.

Trail: Keenan Meadows Trail starts at 4200'. It crosses the South Fork Manastash Creek on a nice bridge, then skirts the bottom of a clear-cut. Head up and cross several roads. At the last road (which is marked) stay to the right for .5 mile. Continue on the trail through two large meadows to its end, where it connects with Shoestring Lake Trail #1385.

Lightning Point #1377.1

Length:	2.4 miles
Elevation:	3600'-5400'
Map:	GTM 240 Easton
Rating:	Medium-Hard (steep)

Trailhead Directions: No trailhead

Other Trails Accessed: 1326, 1377

Trail: Lightning Point Trail #1377.1 is a short and rugged trail connecting the South Cle Elum Ridge and North Fork Taneum Trails. It's a fairly new trail and steep in spots. At the 1.4 mile mark, the trail comes to a road. Stay left on the road around the bend and continue 1 mile more to the top. This last section has a gentler grade, ending at a saddle in the ridge to connect with Trail #1326. It's good for making loops in the Taneum.

*GTM shows it incorrectly as #1377.2.

Little Creek Basin #1334

Length:	4.8 miles
Elevation:	4900'-5200'
Map:	GTM 240 Easton
Rating:	Medium

Trailhead Directions: No trailhead.

Other Trails Accessed: 1326, 1321

Trail: Little Creek Basin Trail #1334 running east and west starts at 4900' and connects Cle Elum Ridge and North Ridge Trails. It begins at an old clear-cut, just below a logging road and descends 2.5 miles down to Little Creek. Go uphill .5 mile to a road and follow it up for one-eighth mile. The trail takes off to the left through forest and meadows. Cross a few small creeks; then climb up to join the North Ridge Trail #1321, where the trail ends at 5200'. There are numerous spots for good trotting in the basin. Active logging in the Taneum may cause trail conditions to change. We've snuck up on large herds of elk here!

Manastash Lake #1350

Length:	4.4 miles
Elevation:	4200'-5500'
Map:	GTM 240 Easton
	GTM 241 Cle Elum
	GTM 273 Manastash Lake
Rating:	Easy-Medium (climbing)

Trailhead Directions: Take exit 109 from I-90 to Ellensburg. Go north on Canyon Road to the Subway and McDonald's Restaurants, then left on Umptanum Road to Manastash Road. Go right on Manastash Road, driving to gravel Forest Service Road 31, then 11 miles more to Buck Meadows. The trailhead is just before the meadow on the left hand side.

Other Trails Accessed: None

Camping: Buck Meadows Campground is just past the trailhead. An outhouse, stream for stock water and tables are available. This is a no fee camp. This campground is scheduled to be moved to the south .5 mile by 1998.

Trail: Manastash Lake Trail starts from Forest Service Road 31 and climbs gradually with some rocky spots. It crosses several logging roads, goes through clear-cuts, and at 2 miles, reaches Lost Lake. Continue south 2.4 miles in forest on several switchbacks to reach Manastash Lake. If you wish, continue up to the ridge. (The trail climbs rapidly.) Loops are possible by returning on Shoestring Lake Trail #1385 and Keenan Meadow Trail #1386. To get to Shoestring Lake, turn right at the ridge and follow the road around, eventually heading north. The views are great of Mount Rainier on a clear day. Stay on the trail marked 4W308 to Tripod Flat. There will be blazes on the trees. (There is a unique bridge made of poles that you'll cross.) Shoestring Lake Trail is not marked. It's on the right-hand side in a meadow. To go to Shoestring Lake, stay on the road for .5 mile more.

Manastash Ridge #1388
(Quartz Mountain to Mount Clifty)

Length:	6 miles
Elevation:	5300'-6100'
Map:	GTM 240 Easton
Rating:	Medium

Trailhead Directions: Take exit 109 from I-90 to Ellensburg. Go north on Canyon Road to the Subway Restaurant, then left on Umptanum Road to Manastash Road. Go right on Manastash Road, driving to gravel Forest Service Road 31, then 11 miles more to Buck Meadows. Continue 10 miles more to Quartz Mountain. Park at the small campground. The trail begins up the road on the right.

Other Trails Accessed: 1363, 947, 948, 1321.1

Camping: An outhouse and table are provided. Bring water for horses and people. No fee.

Trail: Manastash Ridge Trail starts at 6100' on Quartz Mountain and descends on the rugged windswept ridge to the intersection with Taneum Ridge Trail #1363. Along this trail, you have options of taking the easier or more difficult trail. These are posted. Several trails drop off to the left, (south) into the Naches area. There are good flat trotting areas, inclines and declines, and narrow rocky spots, which have great views of some awesome rockslides. At the 3.5 mile junction, the trail continues to the left, west, out to the southern face of Mount Clifty.

Mt. Clifty #1321.1

Length:	1.7 miles
Elevation:	5600'-6000'
Map:	GTM 240 Easton
Rating:	Hard

Trailhead Directions: No trailhead.

Other Trails Accessed: 1321, 1388

Trail: Mount Clifty Trail #1321.1 is a rugged section that has short switchbacks, rock outcroppings and steep drop-offs. The southern part has been washed out due to weather and heavy use. This is a fun trail for the adventurous, with great views. (A mountain goat may even jump in front of you! We're speaking from experience!) We suggest you begin at the north end at the North Ridge Trail.

North face of Mt. Clifty

North Fork Taneum #1377

Length:	15.7 miles
Elevation:	2800'-5000'
Map:	GTM 240 Easton
	GTM 241 Cle Elum
Rating:	Easy-Medium (climbing)

Trailhead Directions: Drive west from Ellensburg, and take the Thorp exit 101 from I-90. Drive south on Thorp Highway 1 mile and turn right on Thorp Cemetery Road. Continue, it becomes Forest Service Road 33. From Cle Elum, take exit 93 Elk Heights, from I-90. Drive the Thorp Prairie Road, paralleling the highway on the north, approximately 3 miles. Turn right and cross over I-90, to Thorp Cemetery Road. Turn right and drive west on Thorp Cemetery Road to Forest Service Road 33. Drive 4 miles more to Ice Water Campground. Roadside parking near the old corral only. You may also pick up the trail at Taneum Junction.

Other Trails Accessed: 1378, 1377.1, 1326, 1367

Camping: Primitive camping only at the Taneum Junction. Trailhead parking is available with an outhouse, and stream for stock water. Be aware that we share this area with motorcyclists. No fee.

Trail: The North Fork Taneum Trail begins on the north side of Forest Service Road 33, just past the Ice Water Campground. The first 2 miles are fairly flat; nearing Taneum Junction, it widens to become an old logging road. Ride up the road 1 mile or so, then the trail drops down to the left (it's marked). Continuing straight is the Cle Elum Ridge Trail #1326. The next 6 miles roll along in forest and through meadows and cross several bridges. You'll junction the Fishhook Flat, Lightning Point, South Fork Taneum Trails and pass the Taneum Shelter. The last portion climbs up and can be rutted out due to heavy use. The trail ends at Windy Pass. Morel and chicken-of-the-woods mushrooms have been found on the trail.

Take It Off or Rake It Off!!

One time, when Rene and I were riding up the North Fork Taneum Trail, we came to a downed tree across the trail. This log was high enough for the motorcyclists to go under, but we were a bit too tall. The log was up a rockslide on one end and across the creek on the other. Rene's mare hollowed her back as she was led under it. I began to lead my gelding under and... crunch! Off went the saddlehorn. We just looked at each other in amazement! Our moral: Take it off, rather than rake it off, even if it takes you half an hour!

Josie

NORTH RIDGE

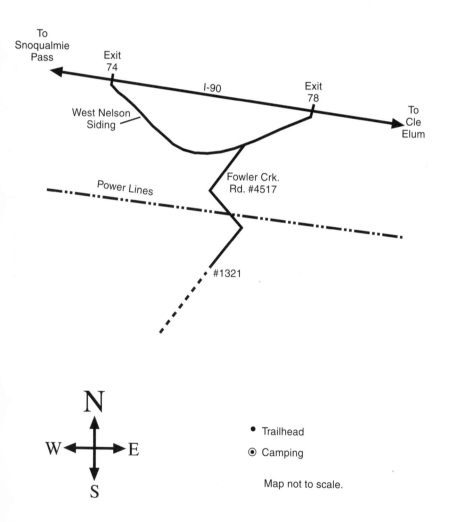

To
Snoqualmie
Pass

Exit
74

I-90

Exit
78

To
Cle
Elum

West Nelson
Siding

Fowler Crk.
Rd. #4517

Power Lines

#1321

N
W ← → E
S

• Trailhead
◉ Camping

Map not to scale.

North Ridge #1321

Length:	9.5 miles
Elevation:	2200'-5900'
Map:	GTM 240 Easton
Rating:	Easy-Medium

Trailhead Directions: Take exit 78 from I-90 and drive south to the first intersection. Turn left across the canal and go right on Fowler Creek. Follow Forest Service Road 4517 to the end. The area has been logged and has ample parking.

Other Trails Accessed: 1341, 1334, 1326, 1321.1, 1326.1

Trail: The North Ridge Trail #1321 begins under the powerlines and switchbacks through forest, then drops into a rocky draw. Water your horses here for water is scarce later. Long switchbacks continue through the forest with occasional views to the west. Several steep climbs will bring you to open bowls, meadows and ridgetops. Blazed Ridge is to the west, where mountain goats are frequently seen. Little Creek Basin Trail joins from the left. You'll crest a ridge where Greek Creek Trail descends, then pass through an old burn. At 9 miles, join Mount Clifty Trail; one-quarter mile further, the North Ridge Trail ends as it connects with the Cle Elum Ridge Trail #1326. Overall, the trail is in good condition with good views on the ridgetops.

*Greek Creek is not shown on GTM.

Greg & Yvonne on the North Ridge

Shoestring Lake #1385

Length:	3.8 miles
Elevation:	4500'-5600'
Map:	GTM 240 Easton
	GTM 241 Cle Elum
Rating:	Easy-Medium (climbing)

Trailhead Directions: Take exit 109 from I-90 in Ellensburg. Go north on Canyon Road to the Subway Restaurant, then go left on Umptanum Road to Manastash Road. Go right on Manastash Road, driving to gravel Forest Service Road 31, then 11 miles more to Buck Meadows. Stay left, the trailhead is 3 miles further on the left.

Other Trails Accessed: 1207, 1386

Camping: Primitive roadside camping or go back to Buck Meadows Campground, which has tables, an outhouse and a fire pit. No fee. Buck Meadows campground is scheduled to be moved .5 mile to the south by 1998.

Trail: Shoestring Lake Trail starts at 4500' and goes to Shoestring Lake. It starts flat, then heads up to the first intersection with Hereford Meadow Trail #1207. You'll immediately join the Keenan Meadow Trail #1386. Continue 1.6 miles up to the lake. The last .5 mile is a jeep road. Stay right on this road. (Left takes you to Tripod Flat.) The lake is at 5600'. Bring the bug spray!

South Fork Taneum #1367

Length:	6.4 miles
Elevation:	3600'-5000'
Map:	GTM 240 Easton
	GTM 241 Cle Elum
Rating:	Medium

Trailhead Directions: Drive west from Ellensburg and take the Thorp exit 101, from I-90. Drive south on Thorp Highway 1 mile to Thorp Cemetery Road, turn right. Continue on, it becomes Forest Service Road 33. From Cle Elum, take exit 93 Elk Heights from I-90. Drive the Thorp Prairie Road, paralleling the highway on the north, approximately 3 miles. Turn right and cross over I-90, to Thorp Cemetery Road. Turn right and drive west on Thorp Cemetery Road to Forest Service Road 33. Drive 8 miles to Taneum Junction. Go left on Forest Service Road 3322, across the bridge and drive 5 miles to South Fork Meadows Campground. The road into the campground is short and narrow. The trail begins at the far end of the campground.

Other Trails Accessed: 1378, 1366, 1363, 1377

Josie up South Fork Taneum

Camping: Three camp spots are available with tables and an out-house. Horse water is in the creek. Bring potable water. No fee is charged at this camp.

Trail: The South Fork Taneum Trail begins at the west side of the campground and can be muddy and rutty at first. Fishhook Flat Trail joins first from the right. Continue through the forest and at 1.5 miles Frost Mountain Trail goes left. The remaining 3.5 miles is fun trail with inclines, declines, and creek crossings in this narrow canyon. Logging has been active towards the top of the trail as it intersects Taneum Ridge Trail #1363, going north and south. Still heading west, go down hill for 1.4 miles to connect with North Fork Taneum #1377, where the trail ends.

*The last 1.4 miles was recently changed from #1377.1 to #1367.

Rene and Josie search for trail.

73

Taneum Ridge #1363

Length:	12.1 miles
Elevation:	2800'-6000'
Map:	GTM 240 Easton GTM 241 Cle Elum
Rating:	Medium-Hard (elev. changes)

Trailhead Directions: Drive west from Ellensburg and take the Thorp exit 101, from I-90 and go south on Thorp Highway 1 mile. Take a right on Thorp Cemetery Road. Continue on, it turns into Forest Service Road 33. From Cle Elum, take exit 93 Elk Heights from I-90. Drive the Thorp Prairie Road, paralleling the highway on the north, approximately 3 miles. Turn right and cross over I-90, to Thorp Cemetery Road. Turn right and drive west on Thorp Cemetery Road to Forest Service Road 33. Drive 8 miles more to Taneum Junction. Turn left across the bridge on Road 3322, then left down the hill to parking.

Other Trails Accessed: 1367, 1388, 1378

Camping: Primitive roadside camping at trailhead with an outhouse, and stream for the horses' water. This camp has no fee. Be aware that we share this area with motorcyclists.

Trail: Taneum Ridge Trail starts west of the parking area and cuts up the side of the hill steadily for the first 3 miles. There are lots of wildflowers in the springtime. The next mile is an old clear-cut and has good opportunities for picture taking. Fishhook Flat Trail #1378 crosses the trail at 4200'. Continue up and over the ridge with mostly good footing, then descend to an open area where the South Fork Taneum Trail intersects. Continue south up Peaches Ridge on well-placed switchbacks that bring you to the ridgetop meadow, where the trail ends. At this point, it intersects Manastash Ridge Trail. This trail can be used in many loop rides in the Taneum area.

"Poor Kathy"

While riding the Taneum Ridge Trail a few years back, Rene and I were trotting along when Rene caught sight of a human skull down an embankment. I volunteered to investigate. What I found was a mannequin head with goggles. There was a light attached, which at one time would have made her eyes flash! The name "Kathy" was written on her skull! We left her there for the next eagle eye to spot!

Josie

Josie on Taneum Ridge

Teanaway

The Teanaway is one of the more rugged areas for riding and offers high ridgetops and steep valleys. This area has few lakes. The Teanaway is fairly dry, which inhabits mountain goats, bear, deer, and mountain lions. The Teanaway is bordered to the north by the Wenatchee Mountains, to the west by Salmon La Sac, to the east by Blewett/Swauk Pass, to the south by Cle Elum. If you enjoy more rugged terrain and trails, scenic ridgetops with great views of the Stuarts, the Teanaway is just the place for you!

Ogan's rig at DeRoux C.G.

TEANAWAY

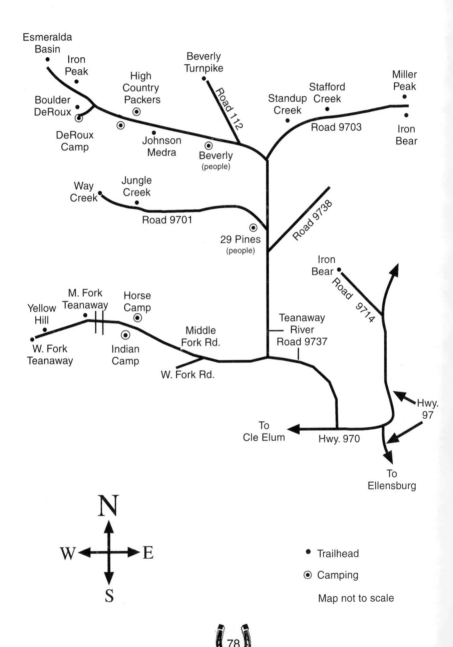

Esmeralda
Basin
Iron
Peak
High
Country
Packers
Beverly
Turnpike
Road 112
Standup
Creek
Stafford
Creek
Miller
Peak
Boulder
DeRoux
Road 9703
Iron
Bear
DeRoux
Camp
Johnson
Medra
Beverly
(people)
Way
Creek
Jungle
Creek
Road 9701
Road 9738
29 Pines
(people)
Iron
Bear
Road 9714
M. Fork
Teanaway
Horse
Camp
Yellow
Hill
Teanaway
River
Road 9737
Middle
Fork Rd.
W. Fork
Teanaway
Indian
Camp
W. Fork Rd.
Hwy.
97
To
Cle Elum
Hwy. 970
To
Ellensburg

N
W ←→ E
S

• Trailhead

⊙ Camping

Map not to scale

78

Bean Creek #1391.1

Length:	3.5 miles
Elevation:	4000'-6400'
Map:	GTM 209 Mt. Stuart
Rating:	Medium

Trailhead Directions: No trailhead.

Other Trails Accessed: 1391, 1369

Trail: Bean Creek Trail begins .5 mile from the Beverly Turnpike Trailhead at 3600'. You'll cross Bean Creek, then ride along the west side of the creek until you reach the upper open meadow, where the trail crosses the creek again. (A side trail heads west to an old camp, then ends.) Climb east up the southwest side of Earl Peak to 6000'. Bean Creek Trail then drops across open hillsides, somewhat vague in spots, down to junction with Standup Creek Trail #1369, where the trail ends.

Beverly Turnpike #1391 (Beverly side)

Length:	3.4 miles
Elevation:	3600'-5800'
Map:	GTM 209 Mt. Stuart
Rating:	Medium

Trailhead Directions: From Highway 970, drive north on the Teanaway Road 9737. Stay right at 29 Pines Campground. Drive approximately 3.5 miles on Road 9737 and go right on Road 112 to the end. Parking is available for 4 rigs with enough room to turn around.

Other Trails Accessed: 1391.1, 1226, 1399, 1215

Camping: Primitive camping along Forest Service Road 112. Creek water for stock. Bring potable water.

Trail: Beverly Turnpike Trail #1391 starts on an old road, then narrows as Bean Creek connects to the right. Go left across the creek and begin a gradual climb up the hillside through the forest, then into some unusual looking rocks. County Line Trail joins at 2.7 miles. Switchbacking up through the trees and meadows brings you to the Iron Peak Trail, then a short .5 mile to the lush saddle at the county divide. The trail enters Chelan County, then the Alpine Lakes Wilderness. The Turnpike side of Beverly Turnpike Trail continues north from here; see the Leavenworth Chapter.

Josie and Rene on the Beverly Turnpike

Boulder DeRoux #1392
(To Gallagher Lake)

Length:	4.1 miles
Elevation:	3800'-5600'
Map:	GTM 209 Mt. Stuart
Rating:	Medium (steep, narrow spot)

Trailhead Directions: From Highway 970, drive north on the Teanaway Road, until the pavement ends at 29 Pines Campground. Stay right on Forest Service Road 9737. Drive to DeRoux Campground, which is on the left, just past High Country Packers Camp. The trail begins at the northwest end of the campground.

Other Trails Accessed: 1392.1

Camping: DeRoux Campground offers an outhouse, nice camp spots under the trees with fire pits and creek water for stock. This is a no-fee camp. Bring potable water.

Trail: The Boulder DeRoux Trail is 7.9 miles long. We are describing the 4.1 mile (east) section up to Gallagher Head Lake. The trail begins flat in forest, crossing the creek several times. You'll junction DeRoux Spur Trail #1392.1 at 4100'. Continue up switchbacks for a short distance as the trail passes narrowly above the rushing waters of DeRoux Creek. Pass through meadows, then take a long switchback up to the lake at 5600'. To make a nice loop, ride around the north end of the lake, then down Trail 4W301, 1 mile or so to intersect Trail #1394, Esmerelda Basin, which takes off to the right, up the hill.

Rene and Tex at Gallagher Head Lake

County Line #1226

(Beverly Creek to Fourth Creek)

Length:	.6 miles
Elevation:	5200'-5600'
Map:	GTM 209 Mt. Stuart
Rating:	Medium

Trailhead Directions: No trailhead

Other Trails Accessed: 1391, 1219

Trail: The County Line Trail between Beverly Creek and Fourth Creek Trails is a short section with switchbacks that climb steeply through open forest. It's a fairly good trail with a few rutted spots at the top.

*GTM shows Fourth Creek Trail incorrectly as #1218. It is #1219.

County Line #1226

(Fourth Creek to Hardscrabble Creek)

Length:	1.8 miles
Elevation:	5600'-5900'
Map:	GTM 209 Mt. Stuart
Rating:	Hard

Trailhead Directions: No trailhead.

Other Trails Accessed: 1219, 1218

Trail: Starting from Fourth Creek Trail, this section of the County Line Trail wanders through open forest on a somewhat rocky hillside. Cross a small tributary to Fourth Creek and continue up as you approach the sandy crest, which is the high point for vistas. The sandy steep trail switchbacks up and with some valiant effort by your stock, you reach the top! Mount Stuart is gorgeous from here. To descend to Hardscrabble Creek Trail, you again have to work your way down a very steep, sandy trail.

I've ridden this trail many times. If you have strong, sure-footed stock and a brave heart, it's a blast!

Rene

Hardscrabble Trail #1218 heading north is somewhat faint.

*GTM shows Fourth Creek Trail incorrectly as #1218. It is #1219.

County Line #1226
(Hardscrabble Creek to Cascade Creek)

Length:	2 miles
Elevation:	5600'-6000'
Map:	GTM 209 Mt. Stuart
Rating:	Hard

Trailhead Directions: No trailhead

Other Trails Accessed: 1218, 1217, 1359

Trail: This section of the County Line Trail, between Hardscrabble Creek and Cascade Creek Trails is vague and seldom used. Leaving the south end of Hardscrabble Creek Trail, you'll be searching for rock cairns or tags in the trees. Ride through sub-alpine terrain and rocks. The trail is hard to follow and is extremely steep with loose sand at the top, which could be washed out. Make your way down across the open hillside on a vague trail to join Stafford and Cascade Creek Trails. ***This is a great challenge for experienced riders and stock.***

County Line #1226
(Cascade Creek to Falls Creek)

Length:	1.6 miles
Elevation:	6000'-6100'
Map:	GTM 209 Mt. Stuart
Rating:	Medium

Trailhead Directions: No trailhead

Other Trails Accessed: 1217, 1210, 1216, 1359

Trail: This section of the County Line Trail between Cascade Creek and Falls Creek Trails, follows along the ridges and sidehills with great views of the Stuart Range and surrounding Mountains. The trail winds below Navaho Peak. It is easy to follow because you are riding across open sidehills.

Deb, atop Red on County Line

County Line #1226
(Miller Peak to Road 113)

Length:	5.4 miles
Elevation:	4500'-5900'
Map:	GTM 210 Liberty
Rating:	Easy-Medium (open hillsides)

Trailhead Directions: Drive north from Ellensburg on Highway 97, past Mineral Springs Restaurant. Turn left on Iron Creek Road 9714, then right on Road 113 to the trailhead.

Other Trails Accessed: 1213, 1364, 1379

Trail: We ride the County Line Trail #1226 from Miller Peak, which goes to Road 113. This section of the trail has fabulous views. Coming off Miller Peak, across open bowls, the trail is wide and has good footing. The view of Mount Rainier to the southwest is awesome on a clear day. The Stuart Range is to the northwest. This trail intersects with Teanaway Ridge Trail #1364 at approximately the 3-mile point. The next 2.6 miles takes you through forest to Road 113, which comes off Iron Creek Road 9714. The ending elevation is 4500'.

DeRoux Spur #1392.1

Length:	2 miles
Elevation:	4100'-5000'
Map:	GTM 209 Mt. Stuart
Rating:	Medium

Trailhead Directions: No trailhead

Other Trails Accessed: 1392, 1393, 1393.1, 1225

Trail: DeRoux Spur Trail starts at 4100' and comes off of the Boulder DeRoux Trail, 1.6 miles from the DeRoux Campground. This trail leaves the forest floor to climb up switchbacks and tops out on the ridge at 5000'. Koppen Mountain Trail

Josie and Rene

#1225 heads south from here. The trail drops down the west side of the ridge on a long switchback to its end as it junctions the Middle Fork Teanaway Trail #1393 and Paris Creek Trail #1393.1 in a lush meadow.

Esmerelda Basin #1394

Length:	5.1 miles
Elevation:	4200'-6400'
Map:	GTM 209 Mt. Stuart
Rating:	Medium

Trailhead Directions: From Highway 970, drive north on the Teanaway Road until the pavement ends at 29 Pines Campground. Stay right on Forest Service Road 9737 to the end. The trailhead is at the side of this parking area. This can be full of hikers' cars, so you might want to consider parking at the DeRoux Campground and riding the access trail.

Other Trails Accessed: 1226

Camping: DeRoux Campground has an outhouse, a creek for stock water, and has fire pits. Bring potable water. There is no fee charged. You can also access Iron Peak and Boulder DeRoux Trails from this Campground

Trail: Esmerelda Basin Trail begins in forest as you ride along the creek. (A hiker-only trail, Ingall's Way, exits to the right at the .4 mile point.) Continue through the forest on long switchbacks; then emerge from the treeline into the upper basin, viewing the beautiful Esmerelda Peaks. County Line Trail #1226 exits to the right at 2.7 miles, heading towards Lake Ann. Stay left and climb to the ridge and gaze at the panoramic views of the glaciers north and west of you! The trail switchbacks down an awesome open hillside for 1.5 miles, taking you to Trail 4W301. If you wish to ride a loop, YEA, walk south up 4W301 trail to Gallagher Head Lake and return via Boulder DeRoux Trail.

Rene above Lake Ann

Iron-Bear Creek #1351

Length:	5.3 miles
Elevation:	3800'-4400'
Map:	GTM 209 Mt. Stuart
	GTM 210 Liberty
Rating:	Medium

Trailhead Directions: Iron-Bear Creek Trail can be accessed from either end. Iron Creek side: Drive north from Ellensburg on Highway 97, past the Mineral Springs Restaurant. Turn left on Iron Creek Road 9714. The trailhead is at the end of the road up a short spur road to the right. There is a small parking area. Bear Creek side: Drive the Teanaway Road until the pavement ends at 29 Pines Campground; stay right. Turn right on Stafford Creek Road 9703, until the road ends. Iron-Bear Creek Trail exits to the east. Miller Peak Trail exits to the northeast.

Other Trails Accessed: 1364, 1379

Camping: Primitive camping available at both ends. An outhouse is on the Teanaway side.

Trail: Iron-Bear Creek Trail is one of our favorite rides, because of the versatile terrain you cross and the loop ride you can make. Beginning at the Iron Creek side, the trail starts at 3800' in beautiful, low brush and trees, then quickly climbs out into the open for great views. Wind up and around two bowls with sparse trees. At the 1.8 mile point, you'll connect with the Teanaway Ridge Trail #1364, heading north and south. Continue west and drop into the thick forest with tamarack trees splashed across the hillside. This last stretch winds down through Bear Creek for 3.5 miles. Boy, can you ever do some nice extending trotting here!

Josie up
Iron Bear

Iron Peak #1399

Length:	3.5 miles
Elevation:	4000'-6100'
Map:	GTM 209 Mt. Stuart
Rating:	Medium

Trailhead Directions: From Highway 970, drive north on the Teanaway Road until the pavement ends. Stay right on Forest Service Road 9737 until .5 mile past DeRoux Campground. The trailhead is on the right side of the road. You can park alongside the road, at the end of road, or at DeRoux Campground (our preference).

Other Trails Accessed: 1391

Camping: DeRoux Campground requires no fee. It has an outhouse. Bring potable water. Stock water is in the creek.

Trail: Iron Peak Trail starts off the North Fork Teanaway Road 9737 and switchbacks up, heading east. It's a beautiful trail with views galore. Well placed switchbacks make a steep climb seem easy. The high point of the trail is 6100'; then it drops down three-quarters of a mile to junction the Beverly Turnpike Trail #1391 at 5600'.

Josie at Iron Peak

Johnson Medra #1383

Length:	6 miles
Elevation:	3100'-5400'
Map:	GTM 209 Mt. Stuart
Rating:	Johnson Creek - Medium
	Medra Creek - Hard

Trailhead Directions: From Highway 970, drive north on the Teanaway Road until the pavement ends. Stay right on Forest Service Road 9737. The trailhead is just past the Beverly Creek Campground on the left. There are pull-offs on either side of the road.

Other Trails Accessed: 1383.1, 1225, 1393

Camping: Primitive roadside camping along the Teanaway Road. Take care of this area; it is used heavily.

Trail: The Johnson Medra Trail #1383 starts at 3100' and goes through forest (with lots of thimble and huckleberries in the late summer). The footing is great as it follows Johnson Creek. At .7 mile, you join Jungle Creek Trail #1383.1. Continue right to eventually switchback up to the ridge; (where Koppen Mountain Trail #1225 is running north and south). Cross over and head down the west side on Medra Creek Trail. **This side isn't recommended for stock.** There are numerous rock croppings and the trail gets steep and narrow with tight switchbacks. Towards the bottom, the trail eases up as it joins the Middle Fork Teanaway Trail #1393, 2.3 miles down from the ridge.

For the adventurous: A great loop is to ride up and over Johnson Medra Trail; then ride north up the Middle Fork Teanaway Trail to DeRoux Spur Trail #1392.1, and finally to Koppen Mountain Trail. Ride over Koppen and Malcolm Mountains on Trail #1225, then down Way Creek to Jungle Creek Trail #1383.1. This is only recommended for experienced stock and riders!

Rene

Jolly Creek #1355

Length:	3.5 miles
Elevation:	3500'-6000'
Map:	GTM 208 Kachess Lake
	GTM 209 Mt. Stuart
Rating:	Medium - Hard

Trailhead Directions: No trailhead

Other Trails Accessed: 1393,1307, 1393.2

Trail: Jolly Creek Trail starts at 3500', 6.7 miles up the Middle Fork Teanaway Trail. (There are some wonderful berry patches here.) Heading northwest, the trail goes through forest for the first 2 miles. At 2.1 miles, an old abandoned trail heads north, up into Skookum Basin #1393.2. (An avalanche occurred here and flattened every tree.) The trail proceeds up to the ridge and is somewhat steep and rough. Once you reach the ridge, head south. (West over the other side, is a game trail.) You will connect with Jolly Mountain Trail #1307 at 6000', where the trail ends. If stock and riders are experienced, you may want to consider a loop, including up the Middle Fork Teanaway Trail to Jolly Creek Trail; then return on Yellow Hill Trail.

Jungle Creek #1383.A

Length:	4.5 miles
Elevation:	2900'-4500'
Map:	GTM 209 Mt. Stuart
Rating:	Medium

Trailhead Directions: From Highway 970, drive north on the Teanaway Road to 29 Pines Campground. Go left on Road 9701 for 2.5 miles. The trailhead is on the right with roadside parking only. This road has been closed at times so be sure to check road closure prior to leaving.

Other Trails Accessed: 1383, 1235

Trail: Jungle Creek Trail begins by climbing 1550' in the first 2.2 miles, crossing the creek several times through the forest. It intersects Way Creek Trail #1235 (going west). The trail declines to the right, switchbacks on a narrow trail, crosses Johnson Creek, and then flattens out to meet the Johnson Medra Trail at 3200'.

Koppen Mountain #1225

Length:	5.8 miles
Elevation:	4800'-5800'
Map:	GTM 209 Mt. Stuart
Rating:	Hard

Trailhead Directions: No trailhead

Other Trails Accessed: 1392.1, 1383, 1235

Trail: Koppen Mountain Trail is described from the north end from the DeRoux Spur Trail #1392.1 at 5000'. Head south up Koppen Mountain Trail. These sections of trail are not maintained and have limited use. A very steep climb will crest at 6031'. What views you have from here! You'll encounter rocky, narrow trail as you ride the ridge. There are sections of loose, rocky hillsides and places where it seems the trail disappears. Then you'll reach Medra Pass. Resting at the pass, prepare to do it all again as you climb up and over Malcolm Mountain. As you reach rocky crests; it seems the trail has no where to go. Just scramble over the ridge to see that the trail does continue! Use your maps to count ridges and search for the trail. After 3 miles from Medra Pass, approximately an hour, you'll reach the junction with Way Creek Trail, which is a much easier trail than the one you just rode. **This trail is for experienced riders and stock only.**

> Bear and bear sign have often been spotted here. I have adopted this trail to make small improvements.
>
> *Rene*

Middle Fork Teanaway #1393

Length:	10.5 miles
Elevation:	2700'-5840'
Map:	GTM 209 Mt. Stuart
Rating:	Easy - Medium

Trailhead Directions: From Highway 970, drive north on the Teanaway Road, take a left on the West Fork Road, then the first right on the Middle Fork Road for approximately 5 miles. The last mile is dirt. We usually park at the Indian Camp Campground or a pull-off on the left side of the road, just before the bridge. The trailhead is on the right, past the bridge.

Other Trails Accessed: 1235, 1355, 1383, 1392.1, 1393.1, 1393.2

Camping: Indian Camp Campground is for people only. You can camp primitively across the road. Bring potable water. Stock water is in the creek on the side of the road.

Trail: The Middle Fork Teanaway Trail begins on a bend just after the bridge crosses the Middle Fork Creek. You'll ford the creek, then wander along an old road, which eventually narrows to trail. Crossing the creek numerous times as the trail follows the riverbed, you'll notice the trail has been re-routed many times due to flooding. At the 3.3 mile point, Way Creek Trail exits right. Continue north on this rolling trail that has some great trotting areas. At 6.7 miles, Jolly Creek Trail heads west from the trail. After a gradual climb, you'll past the Johnson Medra Trail. Continue climbing on what seems an old road, which is fairly rocky. The trail drops off steeply to the left, crossing the creek; you'll see an abandoned trail taking off to the left (Skookum Basin Trail). One mile further, where the trail ends, you'll connect with Paris Creek Trail and DeRoux Spur Trail in an open meadow. This is an easy trail with gentle grades and lots of trotting available. The old railroad bed, which is the trail for most of the Middle Fork Teanaway Trail's length, was used for logging and access to the Skookum Mines in the early part of this century.

Miller Peak #1379

Length:	3.6 miles
Elevation:	3200'-6000'
Map:	GTM 209 Mt. Stuart
	GTM 210 Liberty
Rating:	Medium

Trailhead Directions: From Highway 970, drive north on the Teanaway Road until the pavement ends at 29 Pines Campground. Stay right on Forest Service Road 9737 for 2 miles; then take a right on Stafford Creek Road 9703 to the end of the road. There is a large area here to park and a turn around.

Other Trails Accessed: 1226, 1351

Camping: There is primitive camping throughout this area with an outhouse. It is heavily used and shared with motorcyclists. The Miller Peak Trail heads northeast. (Iron-Bear Trail #1351 heads east from the parking area.)

Trail: Miller Peak Trail #1379 starts at 3200' and ends at 6000'. This is a lush trail as it winds up through the forest, with fantastic views at the top. It begins flat, and slowly works into a hearty climb on well-placed switchbacks. At the top, there is a .4 mile spur trail that leads to Miller Peak for views. If you want more riding (and a loop!), continue on the County Line Trail #1226 to the Teanaway Ridge Trail #1364, then down Iron-Bear Creek Trail #1351. This is one our most enjoyable loops!

Negro Creek #1210

Length:	2 miles
Elevation:	4700'-6100'
Map:	GTM 209 Mt. Stuart
Rating:	Easy-Medium

Trailhead Directions: No trailhead

Other Trails Accessed: 1216, 1226

Trail: The upper section of Negro Creek Trail drops into forest at 6100'. You'll cross several tributaries of Negro Creek in the 2 miles down Road 400. (The lower section of trail is hiker only.) The two sections of trail are separated by 4 miles of Road 400.

Water Lily

Stafford Creek #1359

Length:	6 miles
Elevation:	3100'-6000'
Map:	GTM 209 Mt. Stuart
Rating:	Medium

Trailhead Directions: From Highway 970, drive north on the Teanaway Road until the pavement ends at 29 Pines Campground. Stay right on Forest Service Road 9737 for 2 miles; then stay right again on Stafford Creek Road 9703. The trailhead is about 3 miles further on the left. Parking on the right side of the road.

Other Trails Accessed: 1369, 1226, 1217

Camping: There are many primitive camping spots along this 5-mile road. Be sure to keep stock 200' from the water.

Trail: Stafford Creek Trail begins at 3100' on a rocky trail, crossing the creek, then levels out as you ride through meadows under Navaho Peak. At 4.8 miles, Standup Creek Trail joins from the left at 5000'. Continue up through sparse forest, then into the open, rocky basin to the ridge, where the trail ends. Cascade Creek Trail #1217 heads north, down to Ingalls Creek and the County Line Trail #1226 intersects the trail going east and west. (Riding this trail is a great way to see views of the Stuarts.) A section of trail was washed out in '96 and re-routed up the hill. Again, our Forest Service does a nice job maintaining our trails.

Standup Creek #1369

Length:	5.9 miles
Elevation:	3100'-6200'
Map:	GTM 209 Mt. Stuart
Rating:	Medium-Hard (steep areas)

Trailhead Directions: From Highway 970, drive north on the Teanaway Road until the pavement ends at 29 Pines Campground. Stay right on Forest Service Road 9737 for 2 miles, then right again on Stafford Creek Road 9703 for 1 mile. The trailhead is on the left with parking on the right.

Other Trails Accessed: 1391.1, 1359

Camping: There is no camping in the immediate area, although there is primitive camping all along this 5-mile Road 9703. Use only existing camp spots to minimize impact.

Trail: Standup Creek Trail #1369 begins on an old logging road and takes off to the north on a bend in the road. The trail has a gentle grade at first, then climbs steeply, following switchbacks to where Bean Creek Trail #1391.1 joins from the west. Heading northeast, you'll climb through trees to a high point of 6200', with great views into the upper basin of Stafford Creek. The trail then drops off steeply into subalpine terrain and a meadow. Cross several creeks to join Stafford Creek Trail #1359 at 5000', where the trail ends. There is a lot of great scenery, mountain flowers and wildlife in the area. The trail is narrow a good portion of the way.

Teanaway Ridge #1364

Length:	4 miles
Elevation:	4600'-5500'
Map:	GTM 210 Liberty
Rating:	Medium

Trailhead Directions: Drive Highway 97, north towards Swauk, Blewett Pass. Just past Mineral Springs Campground, take a left on Forest Service Road 9738. Drive approximately 3 miles, past Red Top Mountain turnoff to Road 120, which is gated. The trail begins one-quarter mile up Road 120. Park on the side of Road 9738.

Other Trails Accessed: 126, 1351

Trail: Teanaway Ridge Trail #1364 starts at Forest Service Road 120 at 4600'. The trail climbs quite steeply at first, then levels out. There are numerous inclines and declines. The trail stays in forest and has no drop-offs. At 2.6 miles, you junction with Iron-Bear Creek Trail #1351 (going east and west). Continue north for another 1.4 miles on an open brushy hillside. You'll have great views of Mount Rainier and surrounding mountains. Switchback up and around to a saddle at 5500' to connect with the County Line Trail #1226, where the trail ends. There is no water available on this trail.

Way Creek #1235

Length:	5 miles
Elevation:	3200'-5000'
Map:	GTM 209 Mt. Stuart
Rating:	Medium

Trailhead Directions: No trailhead

Other Trails Accessed: 1393, 1383.1, 1225

Trail: Way Creek Trail is described from the Middle Fork Teanaway Trail. It exits east, 3.3 miles up the Middle Fork Teanaway Trail, with the climb gentle at first, then steepening as you near a road. The trail then heads north, up a jeep trail, which is quite steep and rugged. There are several steep and narrow areas on the trail. At 4 miles, you junction with Koppen Mountain Trail, then drop down 1 mile to where the trail ends as it joins Jungle Creek Trail #1383.1.

*We use this trail to make loop rides in the Teanaway.

West Fork Teanaway #1353

Length:	9.6 miles
Elevation:	2900'-5750'
Map:	GTM 208 Kachess Lake
Rating:	Medium-Hard (narrow, rugged)

Trailhead Directions: From Highway 970, drive north on the Teanaway Road, left on the West Fork Road, then right on the Middle Fork Road. The trailhead is on the right side of the road. We park at the Indian Camp Campground and ride the 3 to 4 miles of logging road to the trailhead, leaving our trailer at Indian Camp Campground.

Other Trails Accessed: 1307

Camping: Primitive camping across from the Indian Camp Campground. Bring potable water. Stock water is in the creek.

Trail: The West Fork Teanaway Trail begins at 2700'. The canyon is quite narrow and rugged. There are several rocky spots and the trail climbs above the creek on the hillsides to avoid the rough terrain. A couple of hunting camps along the trail make for nice lunch spots. As you near the top, you'll ride switchbacks to join Jolly Mountain Trail #1307 at 5600'. It's a gorgeous ride through a unique and deep canyon.

Yellow Hill #1222

Length:	9.2 miles
Elevation:	3800'-6430'
Map:	GTM 209 Kachess Lake
	GTM 209 Mt. Stuart
Rating:	Medium-Hard (narrow ridgetop)

Trailhead Directions: From Highway 970, drive north on the Teanaway Road, left on the West Fork Road, then right on the Middle Fork Road. Drive approximately 5 miles more and park at either the Indian Camp Campground or just before the bridge on the left. Yellow Hill Trail begins on the right, one-quarter mile past the bridge and the Middle Fork Teanaway Trail.

Other Trails Accessed: 1307

Camping: Primitive camping across the road from Indian Camp Campground. Bring potable water, stock water is in the creek.

Trail: Yellow Hill Trail starts at 3700' on an old spur road and climbs through forest up to the ridgetop of Elbow Peak. Water is scarce with one watering spot approximately 20 minutes north of Elbow Peak. The trail gets narrow, rugged and steep. It is quite a challenge! The fabulous views on top are worth the effort. The trail ends as it connects with Jolly Mountain Trail #1307. **We suggest this trail for experienced riders and stock only!**

"Look, I think it's a bear!"

Rene and I had made a loop, riding up the Middle Fork Teanaway Trail, up Jolly Creek Trail, then down Yellow Hill Trail. Things went well until we got to the top of Jolly Creek Trail and weren't sure which way the trail went. We dropped over the west side of the ridge, thinking we were on the West Fork Teanaway Trail, but found out it was just a game trail. I felt a little queasy, so got off to lead. Then my gelding went off the trail. I let go of the rope. He caught his balance and lunged back up the hill. To make sure this wasn't the trail, of course, we went a little further to where the trail was a dead end in a steep ravine with huge boulders. Now we were sure! We proceeded back to the ridge and decided to go out Yellow Hill Trail. There were so many spots that I felt were dangerous on the mount I was riding that day. I got off several times, only to realize the footing was so loose it would be safer on the horse. After all, he has four feet, and I have only two. All of sudden Rene stopped. The trail seemed to disappear as we were perched on the tiptop of a ridge. As Rene calmly sat side-saddle, she leaned over and pointed saying, "Look, there's a bear down there!" I was petrified. My knuckles were white and I felt nauseated. My arms felt like they each weighed 50 lbs. Every inch of movement was forced, even my breathing! That's when Rene noticed that I was near fainting, so moved us on 'till we reached the tree line. Our moral of the Yellow Hill experience: Know that every horse-and-rider team has different needs! Had I been riding my old buckskin gelding I'd had for fifteen years, I would have been more relaxed...

Josie

Leavenworth

Yearly changes are made in the Alpine Lakes Wilderness Area, including the Leavenworth area. Be sure to check with the local rangers for updated information on trail conditions, status of permits, closures and restrictions and designated horse camps.

From Leavenworth, drive the Icicle Road 19.5 miles for access to the Black Pine Horse Camp, which is on the left, one-quarter mile before the road ends. It has approximately 16 drive-through camp spots with tables, water, garbage, fire pits, tie poles and rails. This is a horse-only camp and a fee is charged. Across the road from camp is a stock parking lot with ramp and hitch. You can park here for more than a day. The Leavenworth area has varied riding experiences, from easy valley bottoms to high, rugged ridgetops. The scenery is spectacular on top! Use bear-proof food containers and keep stock at least 200' away from all water sources.

Black Pine Horse Camp

LEAVENWORTH

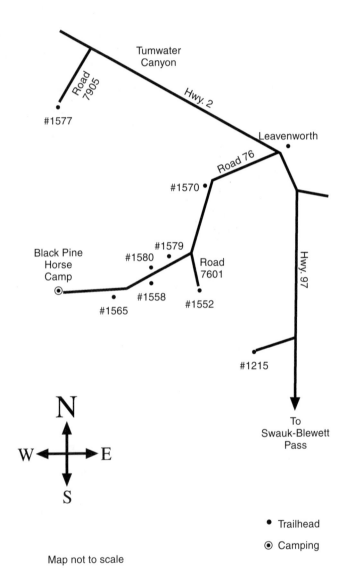

Tumwater Canyon

Road 7905

Hwy. 2

#1577

Leavenworth

Road 76

#1570

Black Pine Horse Camp

#1579

#1580

Road 7601

#1558

#1565

#1552

Hwy. 97

#1215

N

W   E

S

To Swauk-Blewett Pass

• Trailhead

⊙ Camping

Map not to scale

Black Pine Horse Camp

Beverly Turnpike #1391
(Turnpike Side)

Length:	2.6 miles
Elevation:	4800'-5800'
Map:	GTM 209 Mt. Stuart
Rating:	Medium-Hard (steep)

Trailhead Directions: No trailhead

Trail: The Turnpike side of Beverly Turnpike Trail #1391 starts on a saddle on the Chelan County and Alpine Lakes Wilderness boundary. You'll drop down quickly through boulders and steep switchbacks to flatter terrain, taking you to the crossing of Ingalls Creek, which can be very muddy and boggy at times. Cross Ingalls Creek to the end of the trail connecting with Ingalls Creek Trail #1215.

Blackjack Ridge #1565

Length:	6 miles
Elevation:	2800'-6100'
Map:	GTM 117 Chiwaukum Mts. North Central Cascades
Rating:	Hard

Trailhead Directions: From Leavenworth, drive Icicle Road 18.5 miles to the trailhead, which is on your left 1 mile before the Black Pine Horse Camp.

Other Trails Accessed: 1560

Trail: Blackjack Ridge Trail begins with 2.5 miles of switchbacks that are relentless and steep, so have your stock warmed up. You'll travel through forest to reach Blackjack Ridge, then a gorgeous meadow and hillsides. The views across the valley are superb. Traverse below Bootjack Mountain and enter an old burn, which takes you to Pablo Creek Basin. The trail may be hard to find through this section, then will join with Snowall Cradle Lake Trail #1560, approximately 1.5 miles below Cradle Lake. This trail is strenuous in spots, and you may need to navigate. Rene likes using this trail to make loops around Cradle Lake and thoroughly enjoys the challenge. We rated this trail hard because of the climbing, strenuous areas, and the route-finding ability that is necessary.

Cascade Creek #1217

Length:	2.7 miles
Elevation:	3700'-6000'
Map:	GTM 209 Mt. Stuart
Rating:	Medium-Hard (steep, narrow)

Trailhead Directions: No trailhead

Other Trails Accessed: 1215, 1359, 1226

Trail: Cascade Creek Trail leaves Ingalls Creek Trail at the 7.5-mile point. You'll cross the creek and begin climbing through the forest on a somewhat narrow trail. The trail is vague around the meadow area and crests the ridge at 6000', with great views of the Stuart Range. This trail is seldom used and isn't maintained yearly.

Learn about the wildlife you may encounter!

"Ol Griz"

Chain Lakes #1569

Length:	4.5 miles
Elevation:	3800'-5700'
Map:	GTM 176 Stevens Pass
Rating:	Medium-Hard (steep, climbing)

Trailhead Directions: No trailhead

Other Trails Accessed: 1551, 1570

Trail: Chain Lakes Trail starts approximately 10 miles up the Icicle Trail. It exits easterly, zigzagging up through forest on switchbacks. You'll steadily climb for 2 miles more to the mouth of the bowls holding Chain Lakes. The work load is much easier now as you wind past the first lake, then on to the next lake in a park-like setting. Cross an outlet and progress to the grandest of the Chain Lakes. The meadows are stunning. There's always snow above in the rugged peaks around Bulls Tooth. Climb the rocky hillside on a long switchback to the crest. Descend through subalpine forest to reach the end of the trail at Doelle Lake, which lies in a rugged rock bowl. This country is spectacular. It's a lot of work getting here, no matter which way you come in, but it's all well worth the ride. The trail is in good condition to Chain Lakes, although it is steep. Beyond that, the trail towards Frosty Pass is extremely narrow. Please only use this trail for day rides. There aren't sufficient areas 200' back from the lakes for stock camps.

Chatter Creek #1580

Length:	5 miles
Elevation:	2800'-6800'
Map:	GTM 177 Chiwaukum Mts.
Rating:	Hard

Trailhead Directions: From Leavenworth, drive Icicle Road 15.8 miles (.3 miles past the Chatter Creek Campground). The trail begins .1 mile up an old road on the right. It is signed. There is a small parking area here. No facilities.

Other Trails Accessed: 1570

Trail: Chatter Creek Trail starts at 2800' in a brushy clear-cut. When the road and trail split, stay right and begin your ascent. You'll climb 1400' in the next 1.5 miles. Whew! Cross the creek once, while in the forest; then finally enter the open country above. Grindstone Mountain towers above to the west. The stock will be relieved as it levels off a bit. Gaze back south at Eightmile Mountain, Jack and Blackjack Ridges, and Bootjack Mountain, which also have grand rides awaiting you! Prepare to boulder-hop in the upper section of Chatter Creek as you press upwards to the Icicle Ridge. Experienced stock is necessary to maneuver through these rocks. At 5.5 miles, you'll crest the ridge to join Icicle Ridge Trail #1570, where the trail ends. **This is recommended for experienced stock and riders only!** The Forest Service **does not** recommend this trail for stock travel!

Greg at Chatter Creek Trailhead

Eightmile #1552

Length:	3.3 miles
Elevation:	3700'-4400'
Map:	GTM 177 Chiwaukum Mts.
Rating:	Easy-Medium (climbing)

Trailhead Directions: From Leavenworth, drive Icicle Road 8.5 miles and turn left across the bridge to Road 7601. This road inclines 3 miles to the trailhead, where there is a small parking area.

Other Trails Accessed: 1554

Trail: Eightmile Trail #1552 begins in forest, then opens up to vistas near Eightmile Lake. The trail begins climbing partially on roads and is in good condition. It is heavily used, on private land and recommended for stock day use only. Possible point-to-point rides towards Caroline Lakes, Windy Pass and Jack Creek Trails, if 2 rigs are used. There is no horse feed in this area. More ample food is available towards Little Caroline Lake. Stock users may need to tie up near Little Eightmile Lake and hike .5 mile to Eightmile Lake in the future.

Eightmile Trout #1554

Length:	8 miles
Elevation:	4400'-7200'
Map:	GTM 177 Chiwaukum Mts.
Rating:	Medium-Hard (climbing)

Trailhead Directions: No trailhead

Other Trails Accessed: 1557, 1555, 1552

Trail: This 8-mile section of Eightmile Trout Trail is between Trout Lake, and Little Eightmile Lake. Climb up and over Windy Pass, then down to Lake Caroline. The views are panoramic. The trail has a fairly steep grade that lessens as you near Lake Caroline. Horse feed is available between Little Caroline Lake and Windy Pass. Check with rangers for stock camps.

Falls Creek #1216

Length:	4 miles
Elevation:	3700'-6100'
Map:	GTM 209 Mt. Stuart
Rating:	Medium-Hard (vague, steep, narrow)

Trailhead Directions: No trailhead

Other Trails Accessed: 1215, 1226

Trail: Falls Creek Trail begins 6 miles up Ingalls Creek Trail. (Ingalls Creek is usually too treacherous to cross in melt-off.) Falls Creek Trail is a steep and narrow trail that isn't used much. There is a difficult creek crossing about 1 mile up due to washouts. Game trails tend to lead you astray. Use your maps for the number and locations of crossings. There are great views of the Stuart Range at the top, where you junction the County Line Trail #1226, where the trail ends. **Recommended for experienced riders and stock only.**

Fourth Creek #1219

Length:	4.2 miles
Elevation:	4300'-5600'
Map:	GTM 209 Mt. Stuart
Rating:	Easy-Medium

Trailhead Directions: No trailhead

Other Trails Accessed: 1215, 1226

Trail: Fourth Creek Trail begins 11 miles up Ingalls Creek Trail. Crossing Ingalls Creek, Fourth Creek Trail climbs with a moderate grade and levels off towards the upper basin. You'll cross the creek several times. Horse feed is available in the upper portion. It joins the County Line Trail #1226 at 5600'. This is good trail for making loops.

*GTM has Fourth Creek numbered incorrectly as #1218. #1219 is correct.

Fourth of July #1579

Length:	5.3 miles
Elevation:	2300'-6800'
Map:	GTM 177 Chiwaukum Mts.
Rating:	Hard (climbing)

Trailhead Directions: From Leavenworth, drive Icicle Road 9.4 miles. The trailhead is on the right side of the road.

Other Trails Accessed: 1570

Trail: Fourth of July Creek Trail seems to climb skyward endlessly. The only creek you'll cross is at the bottom, so tank up! Endure the ruthless switchbacks as you gain elevation to superb views across the valley. Closer to the Icicle Ridge, the trail eases up to longer traverses across the mountain. At 6800', you join Icicle Ridge Trail #1570 with the look-out one-quarter mile further. Beware! Rattlesnakes are seen on this trail. There are easier routes for you to gain access to the ridge!

French Creek #1595

Length:	11.4 miles
Elevation:	2900'-6100'
Map:	GTM 176 Stevens Pass GTM 177 Chiwaukum Mts.
Rating:	Medium

Trailhead Directions: No trailhead

Other Trails Accessed: 1551, 1564, 1560, 1559

Trail: French Creek Trail begins 1 mile up the Icicle Trail, just after crossing French Creek. This section of trail has excellent footing. At 3.5 miles, you pass French Ridge Trail #1564. Continue riding along as you gradually gain elevation, the Snowall Creek Trail #1560, exits southeast across French Creek. The next 3.7 miles heads deeper into forest, where we found muddier ground. Maintenance here has been low (comment on registers!) and the bridges can be difficult to cross. At 11 miles, the trail connects with Meadow Creek Trail #1559. Head west, uphill, to Paddy-Go-Easy Pass and Sprite Lake. You'll switchback tightly up 1400' in 2 miles. Whew! The views are spectacular; the lake is a short jaunt to the southeast.

French Ridge #1564

Length:	7.2 miles
Elevation:	2900'-5600'
Map:	GTM 176 Stevens Pass
	GTM 177 Chiwaukum Mts.
Rating:	North end - Medium
	Backdoor Trail - Hard (steep)

Trailhead Directions: No trailhead

Other Trails Accessed: 1551, 1595

Trail: The French Ridge Trail begins 2 miles up the Icicle Trail and exits west at 2900'. You'll switchback up to crest the ridge at 5600'. Stop and peek at the rushing waterfall on your way up. The trail briefly flattens, then switchbacks steeply down the "backdoor" section to join French Creek Trail. The views are great and so is the workout!

Josie and Obie on French Ridge

Frosty Wildhorse #1592

(Frosty Side)

Length:	4.7 miles
Elevation:	3000'-5700'
Map:	GTM 177 Chiwaukum Mts.
Rating:	Easy-Medium (steep)

Trailhead Directions: No trailhead

Other Trails Accessed: 1582, 1570, 1551, 1592.1

Trail: This is the Frosty side of the Frosty Wildhorse Trail #1592. The Wildhorse side is in the Lake Wenatchee chapter and has been assigned #1592.1. The Frosty side of Frosty Wildhorse Trail begins 3 miles up the Icicle Trail #1551. This has been re-routed due to a bridge washout. Ride through forest, then pass Lake Margaret and a cascading waterfall. You'll reach Frosty Pass at 5700' with horse camping and feed available west of Frosty Pass.

Unloading at Chatter Creek early one morning, the horses were restless. As I unlatched the pin on the trailer handle, the horse kicked at the door and the wide, flat handle smacked me right in the upper lip, splitting it wide open - OUCH! My riding partner that day drove me into the Leavenworth E.R.. Afterwards, we went back up for a shorter ride and rode into Lake Margaret. Every step reminded me that there would be no trotting that day! Just one of those things that a determined rider puts up with!

Rene

Hardscrabble #1218

Length:	3.7 miles
Elevation:	3900'-5900'
Map:	GTM 209 Mt. Stuart
Rating:	Medium-Hard (steep, vague)

Trailhead Directions: No trailhead

Other Trails Accessed: 1215, 1226

Trail: Hardscrabble Creek Trail begins 9.3 miles up from the Ingalls Creek trailhead. Cross Ingalls Creek, which can be high in early season, and begin your ascent. This trail is steep and doesn't get much use. You need to use your map to count creek crossings and to find the direction you need to go after the crossings. The trail is difficult to find in several spots. Rene likes to make a challenging loop by riding Beverly-Turnpike Trail, down to Ingalls Creek Trail, up Hardscrabble Creek Trail, then up to the County Line Trail and out Beverly Creek Trail. **For experienced stock and riders only!**

*GTM lists Fourth Creek Trail incorrectly as #1218. It is really #1219.

Icicle Trail #1551

Length:	12.1 miles
Elevation:	2900'-5000'
Map:	GTM 176 Stevens Pass GTM 177 Chiwaukum Mts.
Rating:	Easy-Medium (mud bogs)

Trailhead Directions: From Leavenworth, drive Icicle Road 19.5 miles to the roadside parking across from Black Pine Horse Camp. The trail begins one-quarter mile away at the end of the road.

Other Trails Accessed: 1595, 1564, 1592, 1566, 1569, 1582, 2000

Camping: Black Pine Horse Camp is one-quarter mile before the trailhead. Available are drive-through spots, water, garbage, fire pits, tie poles and rails. This is a fee-charged camp.

Trail: Icicle Trail #1551 follows Icicle Creek almost all the way to Josephine Lake. The trail starts at 2900' and is heavily wooded. The trail is fairly flat and at 1.5 miles you cross the horse ford to pass French Creek Trail #1595. In .5 mile, French Ridge Trail exits to the left; then in 3 miles Frosty Wildhorse Trail #1592 leaves, headed north. The next 1.5 miles, you'll wind through the forest, with good footing to the junction with Leland Lake turn-off. The following 2.3 miles tend to be muddy with old bridges. Climb some switchbacks through the forest to the intersection of Chain Lakes Trail #1569, which exits right. The next 3 miles of trail are easy going as you reach the Whitepine Creek Trail junction. This area is more open and flat. The last short climb over a rockslide brings you to Josephine Lake at 4681'. To connect with the Pacific Crest Trail, continue three-quarters of a mile around the north shore of the lake at 5000', where the trail ends.

Josie at
Josephine
Lake

Icicle Loop:
(Trails 1577, 1570, 1575, 1576)

Length:	23 miles
Elevation:	2800'-7300'
Map:	GTM 177 Chiwaukum Mts.
Rating:	Medium-Hard (climbing, vague)

Trailhead Directions: From Leavenworth, drive Highway 2 up
the Tumwater Canyon. Just past the Wenatchee River Bridge,
turn left on Hatchery Creek Road 7905. At both 1.2 and 2.2
miles, the road forks. Stay right at both. At 3 miles, go right
to a small parking area and the trailhead.

Other Trails Accessed: None

119

Trail: The Icicle Loop starts at Hatchery Creek Trail #1577. Immediately begin climbing through brush. At 2.5 miles, views of the Wenatchee River Valley appear. At 3 miles, you pass Badlands Trail #1576, which is the trail you'll return on. Continue left on Hatchery Creek Trail, climbing steeply at times to level off in a nice meadow area. At 6.5 miles, 6700', you will join with the Icicle Ridge Trail #1570. Head west on #1570 into Cabin Creek Basin, where there are several horse camps. At 9 miles is Lake Augusta. Follow Wilderness rules and keep stock 200' back from all water sources. Big Jim Mountain towers above the lake, as you work your way up to the saddle looking into Painter Creek. (You may need to get out your map and do some searching here, because the trail can be vague and there are numerous game trails.) 1.5 miles from the saddle, you'll be at Carter Lake and the junction with Painter Creek Trail #1575. Head north, down the valley, which is a great section of trail through meadows, numerous creek crossings and camps. In 3.1 miles, head east, right, on Badlands Trail #1576, which has several inclines and declines to join you back up with Hatchery Creek Trail. Ride left down Hatchery Creek Trail back to the rig. There is a moderate amount of climbing and searching on this loop, the trail itself is in good condition.

Rene on Sugar

Icicle Ridge #1570
Frosty Pass to Doelle Lakes

Length:	3 miles
Elevation:	5700'-6000'
Map:	GTM 177 Chiwaukum Mts.
	GTM 176 Stevens Pass
Rating:	Hard

Trailhead Directions: No trailhead

Other Trails Accessed: 1592, 1569

Trail: The Icicle Ridge Trail #1570 between Frosty Pass and Doelle Lake is not maintained for 3 miles. A horse camp and feed are available one-quarter mile west of Frosty Pass. It is treacherous riding and the trail is extremely narrow, steep, and rocky. It is very difficult in spots. When you reach the large meadow, continue up and around Doelle Lakes, which are remote and beautiful, with towering rocks above you. The trail is now Chain Lakes Trail #1569. The switchbacks skirting the mountain take you to the crest of the ridge, where you can gaze down upon Chain Lakes. **The trail is not maintained by the Forest Service and is <u>not</u> recommended for stock travel.**

I recommend this ONLY to experienced riders and stock. Crossing this alone with a pack horse the first time, I was quite impressed with the ruggedness of the Icicle! It was very exhilerating and I loved it! So far in my riding this has been the most challenging and adventurous trail!

Rene

Greg on Tomcat

Icicle Ridge #1570
(Frosty Pass to Chatter Creek)

Length:	3.7 miles
Elevation:	5700'-6800'
Map:	GTM 177 Chiwaukum Mts.
Rating:	Hard

Trailhead Directions: No trailhead

Other Trails Accessed: 1592, 1571, 1580

Camping: The Black Pine Horse Camp has drive-through spots, tables, tie poles and rails, outhouses, fire pits, and garbage. There is a fee charged.

Mary's Pass looking west

Trail: The Icicle Ridge Trail #1570 to Chatter Creek Trail heads east from Frosty Pass through subalpine terrain to Lake Mary. The trail climbs hugging the mountain wall and brings you to Mary's Pass at 6900'. Grindstone Mountain is awesomely huge before you and literally takes your break away! You'll feel like you're on top of the world! Upper Florence Lake is .5 mile down. The trail winds across tundra-like hillsides and wildflowers, bringing you to Ladies Pass at 6800'; where Chiwaukum Creek Trail #1571 exits north. Gently guide your stock around the north shoulder of Cape Horn to view Lake Edna below. The trail is narrow, with steep, open country around you. It's GREAT! From Lake Edna, continue down the Icicle Ridge Trail, past the junction with a hiker-only trail. About one-quarter mile further is the junction with Chatter Creek Trail. To access Chatter Creek Trail, follow the trail south across open meadow birches and work your way up the hillside to crest the Icicle Ridge at Chatter Pass. Chatter Creek Trail drops down to the south from here for possible loops. **Recommended for experienced stock and riders!**

Icicle Ridge #1570
(To Hatchery Creek Junction)

Length:	16.5 miles
Elevation:	1200'-7029'
Map:	GTM 177 Chiwaukum Mts. GTM 178 Leavenworth
Rating:	Hard

Trailhead Directions: From Leavenworth, drive Icicle Road 1.4 miles. Turn right on a spur road across from Shore Street to the trailhead.

Other Trails Accessed: 1579, 1577

Trail: To begin Icicle Ridge Trail, take a deep breath, have your stock warmed up and pack lots of water. Start early in the morning for this portion has no mercy! Head skyward, gaining, yes, 1600' in 2 miles! You'll feel a bit of the workload ease as you reach the 6-mile point at 5200'. Ride 2 miles more, enjoying the views; then junction with Fourth of July Creek Trail and the old lookout. This is the high point of the ride. Now drop into Cabin Creek to water the stock and enter a more grassy area. Hatchery Creek Trail, at 16.5 miles and 6700', is welcomed with good feed and possible camps! Lake Augusta is only 3 miles further. It's quite a workout to reach the Alpine Lakes! You'll definitely feel you've conquered something after riding this!

*Most of this trail burned over in the 1994 fires, so it is a very interesting ride to see how Mother Nature is recovering. Riders should expect more logs down over the next 10 years.

Greg on Icicle Ridge

Ingalls Creek #1215

Length:	15.5 miles
Elevation:	2000'-6400'
Map:	GTM 209 Mt. Stuart
	GTM 210 Liberty
Rating:	Easy-Medium (rocky, brushy area)

Trailhead Directions: Drive Highway 97 north from Swauk-Blewett Pass to Ingalls Creek turnoff, which is across the road from the Ingalls Creek Lodge. Stay left after the bridge and drive .5 mile to the trailhead. A large turnaround and parking area with a ramp is available.

Other Trails Accessed: 1216, 1217, 1218, 1219, 1391, 1558

Trails: Ingalls Creek Trail starts at 2000' and follows Ingalls Creek towards Stuart Pass. The trail begins flat, and then narrows as it gradually climbs around a sidehill to meet the wild roaring creek! After about 3 miles, the trail widens. You'll pass over small rock slides, brushy areas, and plenty of sandy spots by the creek, where we often have lunch. The next 6 miles climb through various terrain with occasional views of the towering Stuart Range. At 5.5 miles, Falls Creek Trail heads south across the creek. At 7.5 miles, Cascade Creek Trails exits left with Hardscrabble Creek Trail leaving at 8.8 miles. Fourth Creek Trail joins from the south at 10.3 miles. The next portion of trail is fun to ride through because there are small trees arched over the trail; which gives it a real enveloping effect. Beverly Turnpike exits at 11.7 miles; then you begin a more serious climb through subalpine forest to Stuart Pass at 6400' (just below the west shoulder of Mount Stuart itself!) The trail ends here as it now becomes Jack Creek Trail #1558, which takes you down to the Icicle Road. This is a unique and fabulous ride that has scenery, great footing and splendid views! We watched a whole herd of elk swim across Ingalls Creek!!

Tink, Pam and Josie up Ingalls Creek

Jack Creek #1558

Length:	12 miles
Elevation:	2700'-6400'
Map:	GTM 177 Chiwaukum Mts. GTM 209 Mt. Stuart
Rating:	Medium

Trailhead Directions: From Leavenworth, drive the Icicle Road 17 miles to Rock Island Campground, cross the bridge and take the next left on Road 615. The trailhead is .2 mile on the right with parking for 5 rigs.

Other Trails Accessed: 1557, 1559, 1594, 1215, 1555

Trail: On Jack Creek Trail, you'll ride through a clearcut, cross Jack Creek on a bridge and begin your very gradual ascent through forest, and at 3 miles you join Jack Ridge Trail #1557. Meander on to 3800' to the Meadow Creek Trail junction, which heads west. Still riding on the east banks of the creek, you'll only gain 400' in the next 3.5 miles at which point you join Van Epps Trail #1594. Now in the upper basin, which has limited horse feed, you have only 3.5 miles more of climbing to reach Stuart

Rene up Jack Creek

Pass at 6400'. Overall, this valley bottom has good footing, although it tends to be somewhat muddy in the last 2 to 3 miles toward Stuart Pass.

Jack Ridge #1557

Length:	4 miles
Elevation:	3700'-4800'
Map:	GTM 177 Chiwaukum Mts.
Rating:	Hard

Trailhead Directions: No trailhead

Other Trails Accessed: 1558, 1554, 1555

Trail: Jack Ridge Trail leaves Jack Creek Trail at 3700' on a moderate, steady climb up switchbacks for nice views as you near Trout Lake. You'll drop down 200' in the last .5 mile to connect with Eightmile Trout #1554.

Rene at Mt. Stuart

Meadow Creek #1559

Length:	6.5 miles
Elevation:	3800'-5200'
Map:	GTM 177 Chiwaukum Mts. GTM 176 Stevens Pass
Rating:	Easy

Trailhead Directions: No trailhead

Other Trails Accessed: 1558, 1560, 1595

Trail: Meadow Creek Trail #1559 connects Trail #1558 to #1595. Riding from Jack Creek Trail, head west and at 1.4 miles, Snowall Cradle Lake Trail #1560 exits to the north. Continue on through an inviting meadow with a great horse camp. At the high point of the trail, 5200', you'll skirt around Cradle Mountain to join French Creek Trail #1595, where the trail ends. This is a good section of trail with loops possible.

Rene at Meadow Creek

Snowall Cradle Lake #1560

Length:	9.1 miles
Elevation:	3400'-6400'
Map:	GTM 176 Stevens Pass
	GTM 177 Chiwaukum Mts.
Rating:	Hard

Trailhead Directions: No trailhead

Other Trails Accessed: 1559, 1595

Trail: Snowall Cradle Lake Trail #1560 heads left 6 miles, up French Creek Trail. Ford French Creek and begin the climb up Snowall Creek Trail. You'll gain 1000' in 2 miles. Cross the creek to the north bank as the grade now lessens. Enter meadows and gain awesome views of the 7400' Cradle walls. The trail goes through a mud bog, then makes a hard right. (Don't be led astray by game trails!) Continue on and enter a large meadow; then stay left and switchback up a brushy hillside as it opens up into the enormous upper bowls. The trail passes through a notch in the ridge at 6400' as you can now view Cradle Lake below. Ride down and enjoy some lunch. Leaving the lake, you'll rapidly drop down through boulders to join Blackjack Ridge Trail #1565, heading left. Stay right on #1560 and switchback down through forest, about 3 miles, to intersect with Meadow Creek Trail and the end of the trail. Loops possible.

Cradle Lake, Mt. Stuart to southeast

Whitepine Creek #1582

Length:	8.6 miles
Elevation:	2800'-4600'
Map:	GTM 145 Wenatchee Lake
	GTM 176 Stevens Pass
	GTM 177 Chiwaukum Mts.
Rating:	Easy-Medium (muddy area)

Trailhead Directions: From Highway 2, 14 miles east of Stevens Pass and 6.6 miles west of Coles Corner, turn off to a well-maintained and signed Whitepine Road. Go 3.7 miles to the end of the road and the trailhead. There is a small parking area with easy access.

Other Trails Accessed: 1592, 1551

Trail: The first 2.5 miles of Whitepine Creek Trail #1582 is fairly well used as most the traffic then diverts to the Wildhorse Trail #1592.1 to reach Frosty Pass. Staying right at the junction, now in wilderness, the traffic lessens. The bridge just past the Wildhorse Trail intersection is washed out (an easy ford in summer, but deep and fast in early season). Pass the old site of the guard station and ride through forest, avalanche chutes and meadows to reach the 6-mile point and Mule Creek Camp. Continuing on will be a bit more challenging as the flora thickens. Numerous muddy spots may hinder your travel. Cross another avalanche area through forest to crest the hill at 4600'. It's only .4 mile down to the junction with Icicle Trail #1551. This trail is lightly used and is a route into the wilderness with more solitude than others have.

Trail Notes:

_____

_____

_____

_____

_____

_____

_____

_____

_____

_____

_____

_____

_____

_____

_____

_____

Pacific Crest Trail #2000

The Pacific Crest National Scenic Trail, (PCT) stretching from Mexico to British Columbia is an awesome scenic adventure! Rene's dream is to someday hoofprint the trail completely. Riding Trail #2000 has a certain aura about it. You feel at peace, enriched. We can be thankful that some 70 years ago, the idea was thought of, expressed and eventually action was taken to construct such a grand trail. We've covered several sections from the Goat Rocks Wilderness south of White Pass, north to the North Cascades Highway outside of Winthrop in Washington State. Several sections in Oregon are also covered. As with any other ride, be sure to check for trail conditions, consult weather reports and prepare for emergencies prior to your ride. Enjoy!

Poncho

Pacific Crest Trail   Trail

Chinook Pass		
1.	American Ridge Loop	958, 957, 957A, 958B
2.	North to Crystal Mountain Loop	1163, 1192, 1193, 2000
3.	North to Norse Peak Loop	1191, 2000, 1192, Rd. 410
4.	South to Cougar Lakes Loop	958, 958A, 2000
Deception Lakes North to Stevens Pass		2000
Snoqualmie Pass		
1.	North to Lemah Meadow Trail	1323B, 1323, 2000
2.	South to Stirrup Lake	2000, 1338
White Pass		
1.	North to Twin Sisters	44, 1106, 1107, 2000
	Lakes Loop	1142, 980
2.	South to Goat Rocks Loop	1117, 1118, 2000

● Trailhead

Camping

CHINOOK PASS PACIFIC CREST TRAIL #2000

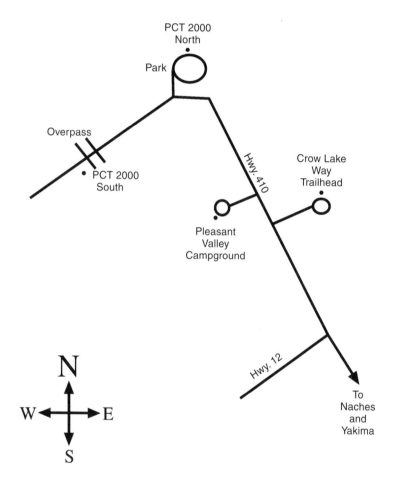

PCT 2000
North

Park

Overpass

PCT 2000
South

Hwy. 410

Crow Lake
Way
Trailhead

Pleasant
Valley
Campground

Hwy. 12

To
Naches
and
Yakima

N
W ← → E
S

• Trailhead

◉ Camping

Map not to scale

Chinook Pass

(American Ridge Loop Trails: 958B, 957, 957A, 958)

Length:	16 miles
Elevation:	3300'-6000'
Map:	GTM 271 Bumping Lake
Rating:	Medium

Trailhead Directions: From Yakima, drive Highway 12 north-west, to Highway 410 (Chinook Pass). Park at the Pleasant Valley Campground. After the summer season, drive 1 mile east to Miner Creek (Crow Lake Way trailhead).

Other Trails Accessed: 972, 959

Trail: Pleasant Valley Lake Trail #958B begins on the south side of Highway 410 and goes flat through the woods to join with Pleasant Valley Trail #957A, which you turn right on. Ride to junction Kettle Creek Trail #957, head left up this trail on some fairly steep switchbacks, and go through forest on good trail to a very small Kettle Lake. Cross several creeks and pass through some wonderful meadow areas that would make great camp spots. Connect with, and head left (northeast) on America Ridge Trail #958. American Ridge Trail travels along the ridges and sidehills with great views into Bumping Lake area. Trail #972 descends to the right, continue on Trail #958. There are a few rocky, loose spots on the trail near the junction with Trail 958B, which you head down. It descends rather quickly. (A short spur trail leads to Pleasant Valley Lake.) Trail #958B takes you down where you began this loop. It's a beautiful fall ride and the views are worth the time spent.

Chinook Pass

(North to Crystal Mountain Loop Trails: 2000, 1163, 1193, 1192)

Length:	24 mile loop
Elevation:	4800'-6800'
Map:	GTM 270 Mt. Rainier East
	GTM 271 Bumping Lake
Rating:	Medium-Hard (narrow)

Trailhead Directions: From Yakima, drive northwest on Highway 12, to Highway 410 (Chinook Pass). Parking is on the north side of the road with a ramp and hitch. This parking area fills up quickly, so arrive early.

Other Trails Accessed: 867A, 967

Trail: Starting on the PCT #2000, head north to rise above Highway 410 on a long switchback with a gradual ascent to Sheep Lake. Traveling along the edge of the lake and through a meadow, you'll climb to Sourdough Gap. Traverse down through open bowls, viewing Placer Lake below. At Bear Gap, 5.5 miles from Chinook Pass, there is an intersection of trails #1193, #967, #2000. Take Henskin Trail #1193 west, left, down to Henskin and Elizabeth Lakes. From here, you'll take Trail #1163, climbing across sidehills, which is narrow in spots, through grassy bowls to Crystal Mountain at 6800'. (Get out the camera, because on a clear day Mount Rainier and the White River make a fantastic background!) Ride cross country east down the bare ski slopes to tie in with Silver Creek Trail #1192, which is up the hill east of the lodge. There may be numerous mountain bikers whizzing quietly down the trail, so be cautious! Water is available 1 mile up at the next junction. Stay left, back up to Bear Gap. Take the PCT #2000 back to the rig. This ride has spectacular views!

Rene near Mt. Rainier

Chinook Pass
(North to Norse Peak Loop Trails: 2000, 1191, 1192, Road 410)

Length:	25 mile loop
Elevation:	4000'-6800'
Map:	GTM 270 Mt. Rainier East
	GTM 271 Bumping Lake
Rating:	Medium

Trailhead Directions: From Yakima, drive Highway 12 north-west to Highway 410 (Chinook Pass). Parking is on the north side of the Highway with a ramp and hitch. This parking area fills up quickly, so arrive early.

Other Trails Accessed: 967, 1193, 1156, 987, 967.1

Trail: The Norse Peak Loop begins on the PCT #2000. It exits from the parking lot, then traverses above Highway 410, through forest to Sheep Lake. The trail switchbacks up through a meadow, then to Sourdough Gap. Ride down through open bowls and sidehills to Bear Gap. There is a major intersection of trails here. Follow the PCT sign north and climb along more open ridges and sidehills towards Norse Peak at 6856'. After passing 3 trails, stay left on Norse Peak Trail #1191 and head down switchbacks into Silver Creek Valley. You'll come out on dirt Road 410, where you turn left and ride up for 3 miles to intersect with Silver Creek Trail #1192 (which is sometimes busy with quiet-running mountain bikers). At the next intersection of trails, water your stock in a stream and stay left on Trail #1192 to the PCT #2000. Ride south on Trail #2000 back to the rig. A great scenic ride that is very popular.

Chinook Pass
(South to Cougar Lakes Trails: 2000, 958, 958A)

Length:	20 mile loop
Elevation:	5200'-5700'
Map:	GTM 270 Mt. Rainier East
	GTM 271 Bumping Lake
Rating:	Medium

Trailhead Directions: From Yakima, drive Highway 12 northwest to Highway 410 (Chinook Pass). Parking is on the north side of the road, with ramps and hitch. This parking area fills up quickly, so arrive early.

Other Trails Accessed: Naches Trail, 968

Trail: Chinook Pass Loop starts on the PCT #2000, heading south out of the parking area. It winds to cross Highway 410, over the by-pass bridge. Traverse across the hillside under Naches Peak on Trail #2000 through a tranquil scene of wildflowers passing Naches Trail. Drop into forest to reach Dewey Lake, with several camping spots available. Stay right on the PCT around the ridge towards smaller Anderson Lake. Take American Ridge Trail #958, which is narrow and brushy in spots, down to Cougar Lakes. Climb up into a rocky basin on Cougar Lake Trail #958A. Join back up with the PCT and ride north, around the west side of the mountain, enjoying the great views of Mount Rainier. The wildflowers are gorgeous through here. Travel through forest and meadows; then cross several ridges back to the saddle, where Trail #958 took off. Stay north on the PCT #2000 back to the rig. This is one of Rene's favorite rides because it's a loop and the scenery is great!

Rene on the Pacific Crest Trail

140

Deception Pass North to Stevens Pass #2000

Length:	17 miles
Elevation:	4000'-6000'
Map:	GTM 176 Stevens Pass
Rating:	Medium

Trailhead Directions: Access from Highway 2 at Stevens Pass or from Salmon La Sac (Fish Lake) area.

Other Trails Accessed: 1060.1, 1061, 1551, 1059, 1066, 1376, 1059.1, 1060

Trail: Leaving Deception Pass, where Trails #1066, #2000, #1376, and #1059 intersect; the PCT #2000 heads north and rounds a bend, then drops into a somewhat small and rugged gully. Riding through forest, you'll eventually emerge onto an open brushy hillside, gaining grand views of the surrounding mountains. Pass a spur Trail #1059.1 that drops into Deception Creek, and continue north on the PCT past Deception Lakes and head uphill to Pieper Pass at 6000'. Head down towards Glacier Lake on several steep switchbacks; then pass several trails below the rugged peaks around Thunder Mountain. Ride above Trapper Creek now on beautiful hillsides down to Hope Lake and at a low 4400' on the Cascade Crest. Still on the PCT #2000, passing Mig Lake (in wet terrain), you'll climb again, passing Icicle Trail #1551. Wind around Lake Susan Jane and cross underneath the powerlines and roads to climb long switchbacks towards the chairlifts. Ride down to the parking lot at Stevens Pass at 4000'.

SNOQUALMIE PASS
PACIFIC CREST TRAIL
2000

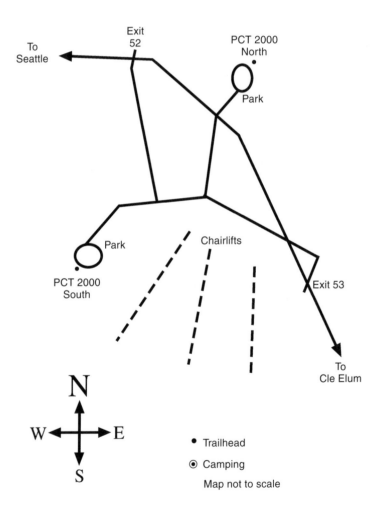

Exit
52

To
Seattle

PCT 2000
North

Park

Park

PCT 2000
South

Chairlifts

Exit 53

To
Cle Elum

N

W   E

S

• Trailhead

◉ Camping

Map not to scale

Snoqualmie Pass

(North to Lemah Meadow Trail - 2 day Trails: 2000, 1323, 1323.2

Length:	30.4 miles
Elevation:	2800'-5700'
Map:	GTM 207 Snoqualmie Pass
	GTM 208 Kachess Lake
Rating:	Medium-Hard (climbing, narrow, drop-offs)

Trailhead Directions: (Described from Cooper Lake south to Snoqualmie Pass as a 2 day trip.) From Cle Elum, drive Highway 903 north, past Lake Cle Elum. Turn right across the bridge onto Cooper River Road. Drive 4.7 miles to Cooper Lake Junction. Turn right; then pass the recreation area and continue 1 mile to stock trailhead, which has a hitch and ramp.

Other Trails Accessed: 1317, 1329, 1323.2, 1323.3, 1331, 1033, 1323.1, 1306

Trail: This two-day trip begins at Cooper Lake. Follow Pete Lake Trail #1323 along the Cooper River, passing several trails. Slowly climb only 200' in the 4.4 miles to Pete Lake, where Trail #1329 heads northeast. (This section of trail is popular and will probably be busy.) Leaving Pete Lake, you'll find Trail #1323 exiting up and over a rocky area, then dropping through forest to cross Lemah Creek. (If waters are too high, you may need to reroute up Lemah Meadow Trail #1323.2 to the right and connect with the PCT #2000 and head south.) Take Trail #1323 left across Lemah Creek and ride through forest 2 miles, passing Trail #1323.3, to join up with the PCT. Three Queens at 6800' is to the south, Chikamin Peak is northwest and to the north is the rugged 7500' Lemah Mountain. Trail #1306 leaves, going into Spectacle Lake. Now you will encounter a more serious set of switchbacks, climbing 1500' up through an avalanche chute to bring you near Park Lakes and a campsite. Trail #1331 joins here. (Mosquitoes may be hanging out in this area, so get out the repellent.) Continuing on the PCT #2000, from Park Lakes to Snoqualmie Pass, there is awesome scenery and some narrow trail. Cresting Chikamin Pass, get out the camera. Rugged mountains surround you! The steep traverse across the southern face of Chikamin Ridge is exhilarating and narrow, so check ahead for oncoming stock. Pass through several gaps; then edge between Joe and Edds Lakes. Climb the north slope of Alaska Mountain and traverse around the rim of the bowl holding Alaska Lake. Pass above Ridge and Gravel Lakes; then climb through meadows, bringing you to the Kendall Katwalk. (This portion of the PCT was blasted across a cliff of solid granite.) It's spectacular to cross. It never ceases to amaze us where the trails are placed. A long traverse around Kendall Ridge drops you into forest passing the Commonwealth Basin Trail. Continue on long switchbacks to the parking area at Snoqualmie Pass. The PCT portion of this ride is 23.9 miles. A fantastic scenic ride!

Kendall Katwalk

Rene at Snoqualmie Pass

Snoqualmie Pass

(South to Stirrup Lake. Trails: 2000, 1338)

Length:	18 mile point-to-point ride
Elevation:	2800'-4500'
Map:	GTM 207 Snoqualmie Pass
Rating:	Medium

Trailhead Directions: Drive I-90 to Snoqualmie Pass and take exit 52 from the west or exit 53 from the east. Go to the parking lot that is south of I-90 and furthest west. The trailhead is in a brushy, flat area west of the ski runs.

Other Trails Accessed: 1303, 1302

Trail: The PCT #2000 starts in brush, then crosses under the chairlifts. Climb through a draw to Beaver Lake. Next you'll come to Lodge Lake; skirt along the slopes and through forest. Climb again, crossing Rockdale creek, and follow a short section of road which you'll cross several times. Cross Ollalie Creek; then ride along Ollalie Meadows. It's a short climb to Windy Pass at 3800'. Descend down a rocky section of trail underneath Silver Peak to a soggy area of tiny ponds. Ride down moderately steep switchbacks to join with Cold Creek Trail #1303. Stay on the PCT #2000. In less than 1 mile, you'll reach Mirror Lake and Mirror Lake Trail #1302 connecting from the east. (We've had wonderful swims here!) Wander along the lake, passing several campsites; then drop down a few steep switchbacks. Cross a road as you approach Twilight Lake. Climb up from the lake entering the forest, cross yet another road and ride through the trees as you pass Stirrup Lake Trail #1338. (Go right .5 mile to view Stirrup Lake.) Turn left on Trail #1338 for .7 mile, which takes you to Road 5484. Go left on Road 5484, then right on Road 5483 for 5 miles, which is a good cool-down for the stock. We use two rigs for a nice point-to-point ride. The drive on the freeway for this 18 mile ride is very short! The views are limited, but the changes in terrain keep this ride interesting.

Terri on the Pacific Crest Trail

Josie & Yvonne dip in Mirror Lake

Twilight Lake

Rene & Yvonne at Beaver Lake

WHITE PASS
PACIFIC CREST TRAIL
#2000

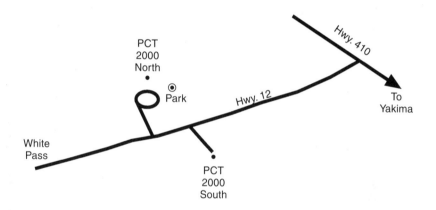

PCT
2000
North

Park

Hwy. 410

Hwy. 12

To
Yakima

White
Pass

PCT
2000
South

• Trailhead

⊙ Camping

Map not to scale

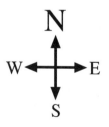

White Pass

(North to Twin Sisters & Tumac Mountain Loop. Trails: 2000, 1107, 980, 44, 1142, 1106)

Length:	25 mile loop
Elevation:	4200'-6300'
Map:	GTM 303 White Pass
Rating:	Easy (steep and narrow on Tumac Mountain)

Trailhead Directions: From Yakima, drive Highway 12 northwest to White Pass. On the north side of the road is the parking area.

Other Trails Accessed: 60, 57, 45, 44, 1104, 980.1

Camping: On the north side of Highway 12, a small camping area is available with an outhouse, tables and fire pits. A fee is charged.

Trail: PCT #2000 begins on the east end of Leech Lake. Gradually switchback up; then level out to junction with Dark Meadows Trail #1107. (This is your return trail, if completing the loop.) Continue on the PCT, 8 miles through forest and past numerous ponds and trails. The footing is the best through here! You'll join Twin Sisters Trail #980, which you ride east on, around Twin Sisters Lakes passing Trail #980.1. Head up Cowlitz Pass Trail #44 and ride to Tumac Mountain at 6340'. The trail is steep, narrow and sandy on the descent down the south side of Tumac Mountain. Ride down to Cowlitz Pass and take the Shellrock

> My boys loved this ride, because of all the trotting and ponds. If you like safe, wide trail and forested scenery, this trail ride is for you. Tumac Mountain is the only area with views and a challenge.
>
>
> *Rene*

Lake Trail #1142. Stay on Trail #1142 to Cramer Lake Trail #1106. Ride down past Dog Lake and turn west (right) on Dark Meadows Trail #1107 to join back up with the PCT, which you will ride back to camp.

Rene and Sugar

White Pass

(South to Goat Rocks Loop. Trails: 1117, 1118, 2000)

Length:	23 mile loop
Elevation:	4000'-6300'
Map:	GTM 303 White Pass
Rating:	Medium

Trailhead Directions: From Yakima, drive Highway 12 to White Pass. There is parking on the north side of the road. There is a small parking area on the south side of Highway 12.

Other Trails Accessed: 1144, 203, 61

Camping: On the north side of Highway 12, a small camping area is available with an outhouse, tables, and fire pits. A fee is required.

Trail: The PCT #2000 leaves the small parking area on the south side of the Highway 12 and climbs through forest gradually, with views of the ski area to the west, passing Trail #1144. You'll cross under Hogback Mountain through an open bowl above Shoe Lake. Trail #1171 leaves, going south to Shoe Lake, and back up again to join the PCT #2000. Continue on out to Tieton Pass, then to McCall Basin (if the snow level permits). Elk Pass is 5 miles further with awesome views. The majority of this ride is in forest on good trail. You'll break out above the treeline at Tieton Pass. The trail south of here into McCall Basin has spectacular scenery and views! To vary the trip back, make a loop down on the North Fork Tieton Trail #1118, then up Shoe Lake Trail #1117 back to the PCT #2000.

Greg on the PCT
above Shoe Lake

Haney Meadow

There are numerous trails in the Haney Meadow area. We've covered the main trails, leaving the side trails for you to explore. Different horse groups have worked on the area, incorporating unique horseshoe plaques on the trees signifying their trails. Check with local rangers for more information. We often haul up Reecer Creek Road, northwest of Ellensburg, to park at Lion Rock and ride to Haney Meadow on one of the spur trails, then ride around Mount Lillian. This makes our loops a more desirable distance! Have fun in this area. Haney Meadow Horse Camp is nice, with tables, tie rails, outhouse, and fire pits. No fee is charged. Horse water is available in the nearby creek. Keep food in bear-resistant panniers or use food hoist.

Josie & Poncho

Haney Meadow Index	Trail #
Howard Creek	1372
Mount Lillian	1601
Naneum Creek	1381
Naneum Meadows	1389
Olds Ellensburg (to Howard Creek)	1373
Tronsen Ridge	1204

HANEY MEADOW

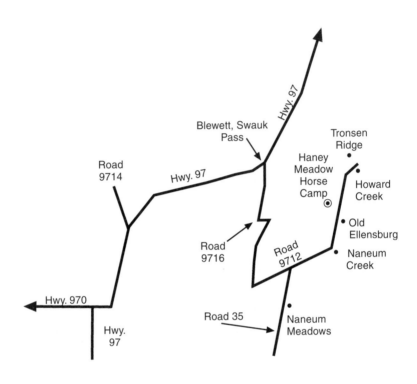

Blewett, Swauk Pass

Road 9714

Hwy. 97

Hwy. 97

Tronsen Ridge

Haney Meadow Horse Camp

Howard Creek

Road 9716

Road 9712

Old Ellensburg

Naneum Creek

Hwy. 970

Hwy. 97

Road 35

Naneum Meadows

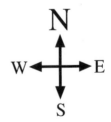

Map not to scale

• Trailhead

◉ Camping

154

Howard Creek #1372

Length:	5.2 miles
Elevation:	5100'-5500'
Map:	GTM 210 Liberty
Rating:	Easy

Trailhead Directions: From Ellensburg, drive Highway 97 north to Blewett, Swauk Pass. Go south on Forest Service Road 9716 to Road 9712. Follow the signs on Road 9712 to Haney Meadow. Howard Creek Trailhead is 3 miles past the Haney Meadow Horse Camp on the right side.

Other Trails Accessed: 1373, 1381

Camping: Haney Meadow Horse Camp has tables, outhouses, tie rails, and fire pits. No fee is charged. Stock water is available in the creek.

Trail: Howard Creek Trail #1372 begins at the 5500' level on Road 9712. Heading south, the trail is fairly flat with good footing. It crosses a creek and goes through old clear-cuts. When you join Trail #1373, stay left. The trail splits again, as Old Ellensburg Trail heads left, you stay right to ride around some awesome scenery. Cross Road 3530 and continue through meadows and over hillsides. Drop down to the Naneum Meadows area, where the trail ends at the intersection with Trail #1381.

Mount Lillian #1601

Length:	1.7 miles
Elevation:	5500'-6100'
Map:	GTM 210 Liberty
Rating:	Medium

Trailhead Directions: No trailhead. Begins .5 mile up Trail #1204.

Other Trails Accessed: 1372, 1204

Camping: Haney Meadow Horse Camp has tables, outhouses, tie rails, and fire pits. No fee is charged. There is camping along Road 9712, past Haney Meadow with no facilities.

Trail: Mount Lillian Trail #1601 starts .5 mile up Trail #1204. Mt. Lillian Trail begins climbing up nice wide switchbacks to some spectacular views of Devil's Gulch. Descend down the southeast side of Mount Lillian to Road 9712 at 5500', where the trail ends. For a loop, continue on the road for one-quarter mile to Howard Creek Trail #1372.

Rene on Mt. Lillian

Naneum Creek #1381

Length:	5.1 miles
Elevation:	5200'-5500'
Map:	GTM 210 Liberty
Rating:	Easy

Trailhead Directions: From Ellensburg, drive Highway 97 north to Blewett, Swauk Pass. Go south on Forest Service Road 9716 to Road 9712; go to Haney Meadow for parking.

Other Trails Accessed: 1389, 1219, 1234, 1372

Camping: Haney Meadow Horse Camp has tables, outhouses, tie rails, and fire pits. No fee is charged. Stock water is available in the creek.

Trail: Naneum Creek Trail #1381 starts off Road 9712, 1 mile before Haney Meadow and heads south. Ride along Naneum Creek through meadows and forest to connect with Trails #1219, #1234, and #1389. At .6 mile more, Howard Creek Trail intersects #1381. Continue 1.1 miles to Road 3530. The trail ends a mile further along the West Fork Naneum Creek, on private land. Many loop possibilities here!

Naneum Meadows #1389

Length:	3.2 miles
Elevation:	5100'-6000'
Map:	GTM 210 Liberty
Rating:	Medium

Trailhead Directions: The trailhead is near a road that we don't recommend for rigs. Access from Haney Meadow or Lion Rock area.

Other Trails Accessed: 1371, 1381

Camping: Haney Meadow Horse Camp has tables, outhouses, tie rails, and fire pits. No fee is charged. Stock water is available in the creek.

Trail: Leaving Naneum Meadows, from the intersection with Trail #1381, the Naneum Meadows Trail heads west and crosses Road 3530. Steeply climb through forest and open hillsides. At 1.5 miles, Trail #1371 heads south. Stay right; continue climbing on good trail to intersect with Road 35, where the trail ends. This is a good access trail connecting with the Lion Rock area.

Brian atop Ali

Old Ellensburg #1373
(To Howard Creek)

Length:	2 miles
Elevation:	5100'-5600'
Map:	GTM 210 Liberty
	GTM 211 Wenatchee
Rating:	Easy

Trailhead Directions: From Ellensburg, drive Highway 97 north to Blewett, Swauk Pass. Go south on Forest Service Road 9716 to Road 9712, then to Haney Meadow. The trail begins on the left side of the road one-quarter mile past Haney Meadow Campground.

Other Trails Accessed: 1372

Trail: Old Ellensburg Trail begins at the far end of Haney Meadow off Road 9712. Head across Naneum Creek and through the woods. You'll climb to a saddle and drop down the other side to open hillsides to intersect with Trail #1372 at 5200'. For a loop, ride either direction on Trail #1372. If you continue southeast on #1373, the trail descends. Then at the end of #1373 at Grouse Spring, take a left on #1373.1 (old 4x4 trail). Continue to Road 9712, then left to Trail #1372.1. (Trail #1372.1 was put in by horse clubs around 1995.)

Tronsen Ridge #1204

Length:	8.5 miles
Elevation:	4400'-5700'
Map:	GTM 210 Liberty
Rating:	Medium

Trailhead Directions: From Ellensburg, drive Highway 97 north to Blewett, Swauk Pass. Go south on Forest Service Road 9716 to Road 9712. The trailhead is one-quarter mile north of Haney Meadow Horse Camp

Other Trails Accessed: 1601, 1223

Trail: Tronsen Ridge Trail #1204 is a moderately steep ridge trail with loose, rocky soil in spots. In about one-quarter mile, Trail #1601 leaves. There is limited water; some areas have been logged. There are great views of the surrounding Wenatchee Mountains. Red Hill Trail #1223 joins at the 4.5 mile-point, headed east. The trail ends in the Ruby Creek area. This is a nice fall ride.

*Tronsen Ridge Trail is noted as TipTop Trail on the GTM.

Rene along Tronsen Ridge Trail

Lake Wenatchee

Rene has done some riding in the Lake Wenatchee area. The trails ridden were thoroughly enjoyed. She recommends this area to you. One of her pack trips begins at Trinity, outside Lake Wenatchee. Endurance rides have been held in this area. Be sure to have maps with you and check with local rangers for updated trail information. Keep horses at least 200' away from all water sources. Have a great ride.

Lake Wenatchee Index	Trail#
Cady Creek	1501
Cady Ridge	1532
Frosty Wildhorse (Wildhorse Side)	1592.1
Little Wenatchee	1525
Nason Ridge	1583

LAKE WENATCHEE

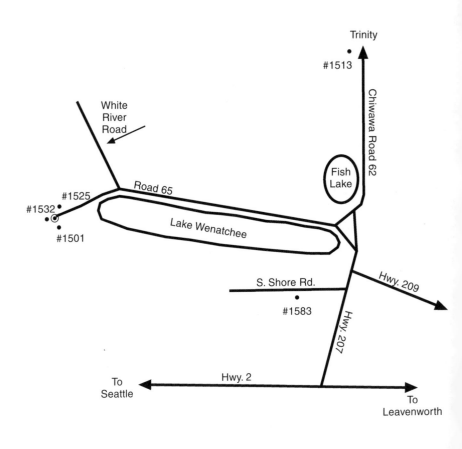

Trinity

• #1513

Chiwawa Road 62

White
River
Road

Fish
Lake

Road 65

#1525 •
#1532 • ⊙
#1501 •

Lake Wenatchee

Hwy. 209

S. Shore Rd.

• #1583

Hwy. 207

Hwy. 2

To
Seattle

To
Leavenworth

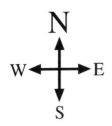

N

W ◄───► E

S

• Trailhead

⊙ Camping

Map not to scale

Cady Creek #1501

Length:	5 miles
Elevation:	3000'-4300'
Map:	GTM 144 Benchmark Mtn.
Rating:	Easy-Medium (muddy)

Trailhead Directions: From Leavenworth, drive Highway 2 west towards Stevens Pass, about 16 miles. At Coles Corner (gas station), go north on Highway 207. Drive along the North Shore of Lake Wenatchee and turn left on Road 65 (approximately 15 miles). Go to the end of the road to the trailhead.

Other Trails Accessed: 1532, 2000, 1520, 1525

Trail: Cady Creek Trail begins at 3000' and heads northwest. (Cady Creek Trail shares the same trailhead with Trail #1525 and #1520.) Cady Ridge Trail exits in .5 mile. Stay left, following Cady Creek Trail through the valley bottom, which is quite brushy and muddy. This trail takes you to the PCT #2000 at Cady Pass in 5 miles. There are lots of berries along the way too! Loops are possible.

Cady Ridge #1532

Length:	6 miles
Elevation:	3000'-5800'
Map:	GTM 144 Benchmark Mtn.
Rating:	Medium-Hard
	(upper part steep, rugged)

Trailhead Directions: No trailhead, it starts .5 mile up Cady Creek Trail.

Other Trails Accessed: 1501, 2000

Trail: Cady Ridge Trail #1532 begins off Cady Creek Trail, .5 mile from the trailhead (Little Wenatchee Ford Campground). It is quite steep and there is little or no water available. If you are considering using this trail in a loop ride, we recommend you first warm up your horse. The trail connects with the PCT #2000 near Lake Sally Ann. **We suggest this trail for experienced stock and riders only!** Please, no stopping or camping with stock at Lake Sally Ann. No campfires are allowed in Lake Sally Ann Basin. Good alternative camps are in Foggy Basin, north to Cady Pass, and at Meander Meadow and Indian Pass.

Frosty Wildhorse #1592.1
(Wildhorse Side)

Length:	6.6 miles
Elevation:	3200'-5700'
Map:	GTM 177 Chiwaukum Mts.
Rating:	Medium

Trailhead Directions: No trailhead.

Other Trails Accessed: 1592, 1570, 1582

Trail: The Wildhorse side of Frosty Wildhorse Trail is assigned #1592.1. The trail leaves from the Lake Wenatchee area, heads south and leaves Whitepine Trail #1582 at the 2-mile point. Enter into the Alpine Lake Wilderness and ride through mostly shrub and huckleberry bushes on the north side of Frosty Pass. A fire has wiped out virtually all the trees in the valley. Although this can be a sun-blazed trail in mid-season, the side streams keep ample water available for your stock. You begin switchbacking up through forest, then enter a vast valley of brush to view the Chiwaukum Mountains above, with Grace Lake tucked neatly in. The spur trail to Grace Lake is not maintained and is closed to stock. It is a short walk from an old sheep herder camp. The trail then crosses a ridge at 5200' to continue underneath Snowgrass Mountain towering overhead. Frosty Pass is reached at 5700'. The trail is now Frosty Trail. The trail, the main route to Frosty Pass, gets moderate to heavy use. Horse camping and feed are available west of Frosty Pass.

*The trail section south of Frosty Pass is Frosty Trail #1592. The north part, in the Lake Wenatchee District, is Wildhorse Trail #1592.1.

Little Wenatchee #1525

Length:	7 miles
Elevation:	3000'-5500'
Map:	GTM 144 Benchmark Mtn.
Rating:	Easy-Medium (steep near PCT)

Trailhead Directions: From Leavenworth, drive Highway 2 west towards Stevens Pass, about 16 miles. At Coles Corner (gas station), go north on Highway 207. Drive along the North Shore of Lake Wenatchee and turn left on Road 65 (approximately 15 miles). Go to the end of the road to the trailhead.

Other Trails Accessed: 1520, 1501, 2000

Trail: Little Wenatchee Trail shares the same trailhead with Trails #1520 and #1501. It heads north through the valley bottom, along the creek, crossing it several times. After 4.5 miles, you rise up closer to Meander Meadow, under Kodak Peak. Meander Meadow is often quite boggy. A good camp is in lower Meander Meadow; it has better feed. The last section is fairly steep and washed out as you join the PCT #2000. It's a good trail to use for loops in this area.

Nason Ridge #1583

Length:	24 miles
Elevation:	2000'-6200'
Map:	GTM 145 Wenatchee Lake
	GTM 146 Plain
Rating:	Hard

Trailhead Directions: Drive Highway 2 west from Leavenworth to Coles Corner (towards Stevens Pass, approximately 16 miles). Take Highway 207 north, then go left at the Nason Creek Campground to the trailhead.

Other Trails Accessed: 1529, 1588, 1587, 1583A

Trail: Nason Ridge Trail is a scenic trail out across Nason Ridge; with views of Lake Wenatchee. At about 6 miles, Trail #1529 exits. (The first 9 miles is open to motorcyclists, but not past the Alpine Lookout.) At the 9-mile point, Trail #1583A leaves; then Trail #1588 exits in 1 mile more. The next 5 miles of good ridge riding brings you to Royal Basin, where for 3 miles it **isn't recommended for stock!** Trail #1587 leaves, going south (just past Rock Lake). The remaining 3 miles take you down to Snowy Creek and the end of the trail at Road 6700. A point-to-point ride is possible with 2 rigs. A shorter point-to-point trip could be ridden by using the Merrit Lake Trail #1588, which has a loading ramp at that trailhead. **The middle section is recommended for experienced stock and riders only!**

Rene on Nason Ridge

Stehekin and Pasayten Pack Trips

Rene, Greg and their three boys have been packing several years and continue to explore new wilderness areas. They love the challenge of leaving the rig and being totally dependent on their knowledge and skills of stock and the outdoors. Packing is a great family sport for them. Use bear-proof panniers or a food hoist and keep stock at least 200' back from all water sources.

Stehekin Pack Trips:	
1. Rainy Pass to Stehekin (6 day loop)	PCT 200
	McAlester
	Rainbow
	Rainbow Loop
	Stehekin Valley Road
	Stellito Spur
2. Trinity to Rainy Pass	1513
(6 day point-to-point)	789
	2000
3. McGregor Mountain	No Number

PASAYTEN
WILDERNESS

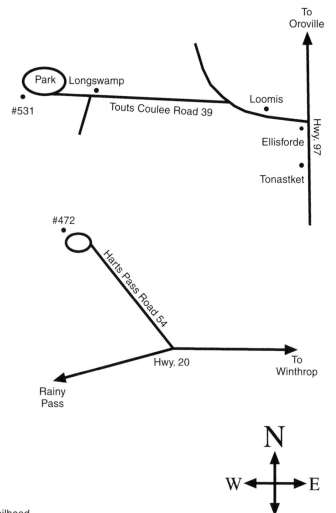

To
Oroville

Park   Longswamp

#531

Touts Coulee Road 39

Loomis

Hwy. 97

Ellisforde

Tonastket

#472

Harts Pass Road 54

Hwy. 20

To
Winthrop

Rainy
Pass

N

W   E

S

• Trailhead

◉ Camping

Map not to scale

169

Pasayten: Longswamp to Tungsten (5 day loop)
Trails: 531, 362, 342, 533, 534, 510

Length:	40 miles
Elevation:	4400'-7800'
Map:	GTM 20 Coleman Peak
	GTM 21 Horseshoe Basin
Rating:	Medium

Trailhead Directions: Drive Highway 97 north from Tonasket to Ellisforde. Turn left across the river to County Road 9437; then drive Road 9425 to Loomis. Two miles out of Loomis, turn left on Touts Coulee Road 39. Follow it 20 miles to Longswamp; then stay right until the road ends at the trailhead. There is parking for 5 rigs, with a ramp and hitch.

*GTM shows Road 39 as 390

Other Trails Accessed: 561, 360, 375, 533.D, 340

Rene at Windy Peak

Trail: To begin the 5 day Pasayten Loop, head down Chewack Driveway Trail #531; immediately take a right up Trail #362, climbing through forest and meadows. The upper portion of the trail is vague as you ride on an open, rocky hillside to reach Windy Peak at 7800' to join the Windy Creek Trail. There is a small sign at the top to guide you. Now on Trail #342, head north and enjoy the views of the Eastern Pasayten. Wind around Topaz Mountain; then drop down to meet the Boundary Trail #533 with camp spots near. Ride west on the Boundary Trail #533 towards Louden Lake and more camp spots. Continue on #533 under Teapot Dome, to Scheelite

Pass at 6700'. Ride 3 miles to join with Tungsten Trail #534 and a camp area. Travel south down Tungsten Trail #534 through the drainage and along the creek bottom, with several nice horse camps. Trail #534 ends at the junction with Trail #510. Continue south on Chewack Trail #510 through the valley bottom, passing several trails to connect with Chewack Driveway Trail #531. Climb east on #531, up steep switchbacks; then the trail levels out as you return to the rig. Rene and a girlfriend made this trip one fall and thought it was spectacular.

Pasayten: Longswamp to Slate Pass (10 day point-to point)
(Trails: 531, 510, 534, 533, 502, 451, 477, 478, 472)

Length:	80 miles
Elevation:	4000'-7800'
Map:	GTM 18 Pasayten Peak
	GTM 19 Billy Goat Mtn.
	GTM 20 Coleman Peak
	GTM 21 Horseshoe Basin
	GTM 50 Washington Pass
Rating:	Medium

Trailhead Directions: Drive Highway 97 north from Tonasket to Ellisforde, Turn left and cross the river to County Road 9437. Follow Roads 9437 and 9425 to Loomis. Go through Loomis, 2 miles north of town turn left on Touts Coulee Road 39. Follow Road 39 for 20 miles to Longswamp. At the fork, stay right until the road ends at the trailhead. Parking is available for 5 rigs, with ramp and hitches.

Heading Down
McCall Gulch

Other Trails Accessed: 362, 561, 360, 565, 545, 504, 500, 529, 473, 502C, 461, 451A, Lower Cathedral Lake, 510, Whistler Basin, 456, 454, 472A.

Trail: The Pasayten 10-day, point-to-point ride begins by heading down Chewack Driveway Trail #531, passing Trail #362, then through the forest as rather steep switchbacks take you down to join the Chewack Trail #510, which you head north on, and pass several side trails. (This is a nice, scenic valley trail with a lot of fishing holes and several good horse camps.) At 6 miles, head up Tungsten Trail #534. Ride through forest, on sidehills, and through meadow areas to connect with the Boundary Trail #533, turn left (west). (There are camps 1 mile further, left towards Apex Pass.) At Apex Pass, 7800', your views east and west are grand! Continue on #533, riding on sidehills towards Cathedral Peak. (Look carefully, for you may see some courageous rock climbers!) Pass Cathedral Lakes and 5 trails, bringing you to some nice meadows; and head down to the Ashnola River to Trail #500 and a good camp spot. Sheep Mountain and Meadows are just up the hill for other camping. Continue out the Boundary Trail to Peevee Pass, and head south on Larch Creek Trail #502. Ride through large, open bowls and across ridges with fantastic scenery for great camera shots, you'll pass Trails #502C and Whistler Basin. Head down from the ridge into McCall Gulch on the East Fork Pasayten Trail #451, now entering forest. Trail #451A joins, keep right, still on #451. Follow the river down on good trail to the north end of Big Hidden lake to a camp spot. There is a lean-to and creek, but no feed. (The fishing is good here, so get out the frying pan!) This is the junction with Trail #477. Head north on #477, down the East Fork Pasayten to join with the Boundary Trail #533 again, which you head south on, passing many creeks and trails. At the next junction with #478, ride left on Trail #478, and pass through the old airstrip, which has a lot of feed in this long meadow. Ride out the south end of the airstrip to the next junction. Stop and get out the maps! There are numerous different routes here. Rene's family ventured out on the West Fork Pasayten Trail #472 through 10 miles of forest, and meadows with good camping spots. Cross the creek for the last time, and begin the climb up the hillside to emerge from the treeline, YEA!

South towards Slate Peak

Looking south, you can see Slate Peak awaiting your arrival. The PCT #2000 is traversing the ridges to the west and Haystack Mountain is towering above you. Long switchbacks through a large rock slide brings you to Slate Peak at 7200'. There was still a large snow bank here when we arrived. Rene's Fjord horse willingly took the lead to test the footing. Nice, firm snow in August, thank goodness! The Pasayten is beautiful country. Rene's family varies their pack trips. Most often, they pack in to a base camp, but have also moved camp daily. Either way, it's a fun trip.

STEHEKIN

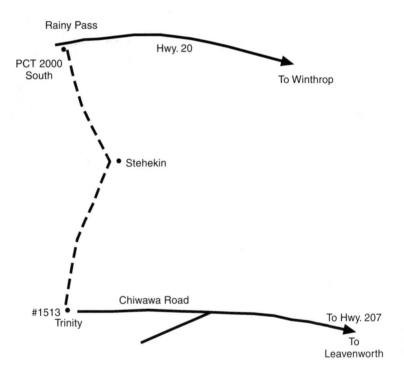

Rainy Pass

Hwy. 20

PCT 2000
South

To Winthrop

• Stehekin

Chiwawa Road

#1513 •
Trinity

To Hwy. 207

To
Leavenworth

N

W ← → E

S

• Trailhead

◉ Camping

Map not to scale

Stehekin: Rainy Pass to Stehekin (6 day loop)

(Trails: 2000, McAlester, Stilleto Spur, Rainbow, Rainbow Loop, Stehekin Valley Road.

Length:	45 miles
Elevation:	1200'-6000'
Map:	GTM 50 Washington Pass GTM 81 McGregor Mtn. GTM 82 Stehekin
Rating:	Easy-Medium (climbing)

Trailhead Directions: Drive Highway 20 from Winthrop to Rainy Pass. Parking is available on the north side of the highway. There is an outhouse available.

Other Trails Accessed: South Pass, Rainbow Lake, Walker Park, Twisp Pass, McGregor Mountain, Stilleto Peak, 426

Trail: Rainy Pass Loop begins by heading south on the PCT #2000 through forest on an easy trail. Either take the Stilleto Spur Trail left to McAlester Trail, or continue on the PCT #2000 south to Fireweed camps. Cross to McAlester Trail, passing Twisp Pass Trail. Ride up McAlester Trail 4 miles to McAlester Lake for a great horse camp. When leaving here, continue up to McAlester

Packed and ready at Rainy Pass!

175

Pass at 6000'; where South Pass Trail and Rainbow Creek Trail meet. Drop into Rainbow Creek Trail for 8 miles on a nice, wide trail. Cross the creek several times, passing Rainbow Lake Trail to intersect Rainbow Loop Trail, which you take to the right. This will drop you out onto the Stehekin Valley Road, turn right. Ride 4.5 miles to a lodging point. Having made prior arrangements, Ogans have stayed at the Stehekin Valley Ranch several times. The Courtney family, who run the Cascade Corrals, know the true meaning of hospitality! There is also a horse camp at Bridge Creek. Return to Rainy Pass on the PCT #2000, north from High Bridge, through forest, with great views of the valley as you are on open hillsides a lot of the way. You'll pass McGregor Mountain Trail, Walker Park Trail, and Rainbow Lake Trail. Several horse camps are available north of Bridge Creek on the PCT. This was a really great trip; the Ogan boys especially loved McAlester Lake.

Ogans crossing Bridge Creek

Stehekin: Trinity to Rainy Pass (6 day point-to-point)
(Trails: 1513, 789, 2000)

Length:	58 miles
Elevation:	1700'-6200'
Map:	GTM 50 Washington Pass
	GTM 81 McGregor Mtn.
	GTM 82 Stehekin
	GTM 113 Holden
Rating:	Medium

Trailhead Directions: Drive Highway 2 from Leavenworth to Coles Corner. Take Highway 207 and at the fork in the road, stay right on Chiwawa Loop Road 62. Follow Trinity signs to the end of the road and the trailhead. Chiwawa Horse Camp is available.

Other Trails Accessed:
1550, 792, 785, 1242, 1272, 1279, 1239, 1562.2, 799, 787, 426, 1256, Walker Park, Rainbow Lake, McAlester, Stilleto Spur, McGregor Mountain, Cascade Horse Trail, Agnes Gorge

Greg on PCT

Trail: The Stehekin 6 day point-to-point trip begins at Trinity. Ride past houses (which are on private property) on an old road, where Trail #1513 begins. At 1.4 miles, Trail #1550 exits, ride 10 miles through open valleys and meadows to Buck Creek Pass. There is a horse camp at the pass. Views of Glacier Peak are spectacular! Leave Buck Creek Pass to cross the Middle Ridge on Buck Pass Trail #789, heading northwest, which is narrow and brushy, going down the hillside. When you enter forest, the trail is wide and has good footing as you join up with the PCT #2000. Head north, right, crossing Miners Creek, then turn right and climb to Suiattle Pass at 5983'. Here Trail #1279 comes in, continue north on the PCT. (There are great views of Cloudy Peak to the east.) Switchback down through a boulder field, then wind in and out of several deep side canyons, dropping into Agnes Creek, where there is a small camp. PCT #2000 follows the valley bottom, passing numerous campsites and trails. You'll cross a bridge nearing Agnes Creek Gorge. (The Forest Service has a corral at High Bridge, which the Ogans have stayed at. Check ahead with local Forest Service for arrangements. Another option is to contact the Courtney family in Stehekin for a unique stay at the Stehekin Valley Ranch, just a couple of miles down Stehekin Valley Road. Write to them at: The Courtney Family, P.O. Box 67, Stehekin, WA 98852.) 5 miles further up the PCT from High Bridge is the Bridge Creek Horse Camp. The last leg of this eventful trip takes you north from Bridge Creek Camp on the PCT through meadows, forest and sidehills. The trails you'll pass are: Cascade Horse Trail, McGregor Mountain Trail, Walker Park Trail, Rainbow Lake Trail, McAlester Trail, and Stilleto Spur Trail. There are several horse camps available along this 17-mile stretch to Rainy Pass. The views on this trip are awesome, the trail is in good condition and the experience is great!

Rene atop the Middle Ridge

Glacier Peak from Buck Pass

McGregor Mountain

Length:	7.3 miles
Elevation:	1500'-8000'
Map:	GTM 81 McGregor Mtn.
Rating:	Hard

Trailhead Directions: No trailhead.

Other Trails Accessed: PCT #2000

Trail: McGregor Mountain Trail begins from the PCT #2000, 1 mile north of High Bridge, just past Coon Lake. Begin climbing through forest, then subalpine terrain. After 4 miles, you'll enter an open, rocky basin with views unlimited. The switchbacks will lengthen out now as you've followed Coon Creek upwards, only hearing it a few times. At 6.6 miles, you reach Heaton Camp, an old camp at which many will feel they have ventured far enough! For the adventurous, continue upwards on what now seems like a trail for the mountain goats! Ride one-quarter mile to a rocky bluff, where the stock actually can't go any further. There is nothing to tie your horse to, if this gives you a clue to your surroundings! The switchbacks are relentless on this ride; the last portion is narrow, and...imagine the panoramic view at 8000'! For the hikers, look for the black arrow painted on the rocks, signifying the route up through the crevice to where the old lookout used to be at 8122'.

Rene ventured out on her own, as her family got some R&R for a day at the Stehekin Valley Ranch. She thought this was quite an exhilarating experience by herself!

Mindful stock is a must in the mountains

I thrive on Hellatious Trails!
−Tex

Oregon: Bull of the Woods Wilderness

The Bagby Trail is the only trail described in this section. (Although more trails were ridden, there were too many logs down to finish them.) The road to the trailhead is **very steep.** Josie is sure that's why nobody was up there! The forest is dense and the views from the ridges are awesome. (Water is always available.) Heading towards the Bagby Hot Springs, you will sense civilization again. You moved from one extreme to the other. This is a rugged area that may not be for everyone, although Josie enjoyed it.

Blaze on...

Josie and Bandit on the Bagby Trail

Riding the ridge on Bagby Trail

Trail Notes:

_____

_____

_____

_____

_____

_____

_____

_____

_____

_____

_____

BULL OF THE WOODS

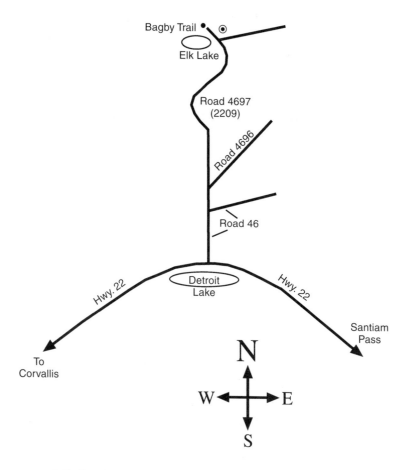

Bagby Trail

Elk Lake

Road 4697
(2209)

Road 4696

Road 46

Detroit
Lake

Hwy. 22

Hwy. 22

Santiam
Pass

To
Corvallis

N
W ← → E
S

● Trailhead

◉ Camping

Map not to scale

183

Bagby #544 (to Bagby Hot Springs)

Length:	10 miles
Elevation:	4000'-4600'
Map:	GTM 524 Battle Ax
Rating:	Medium (climbing, narrow)

Trailhead Directions: Heading west off Santiam Pass, turn right on Road 46 at Detroit Lake. Turn left at Road 4697 (2209 on GTM). This is a washboardy, dusty, very steep road that is **not recommended for trailers.** Elk Lake and Dunlop Lake are near the top. There is a small turnout before the road turns left toward the lakes. This is the only place to park. The road leading toward the lakes is 4WD.

Other Trails Accessed: 573, 546

Camping: Primitive camping is available at a small turnout before the road turns toward the lakes. The last section is a jeep road and is **not** for trailers! Stock water is available at Dunlop Lake.

Trail: The Bagby Trail begins at beautiful Elk Lake and goes into Bagby Hot Springs. The trail switchbacks up the north side of Elk Lake on a narrow path through brush and rocks. Ride a ridge; the trail then flattens out as you join Twin Lakes Trail #573. Wind around a narrow hillside on the shoulder of Silver King Mountain atop a ridge, which intersects Trail #546. Stay on Trail #544, and switchback down toward Bagby Hot Springs in dense forest. (Josie and a friend were on the lookout for elves as they were sure they lived close!) There was one tricky spot, where the trail had been eroded, about 1 mile before the hot springs. Logs were down, so consider bringing a small saw. The rocky ridgetops and deep, hazy valleys of late summer were great. The hot springs are very enjoyable as "The Friends of Bagby" maintain them. There is a cabin occupied by the caretaker. You get a choice of a big communal hot tub or smaller private log tub. You may be nude here! The springs may also be accessed from Bagby Road 70. There was no fee charged.

Oregon: Mt. Jefferson Wilderness

The Mount Jefferson area has some of the most awesome and well-maintained trails Josie has been on. The footing was great, the lakes were clean and clear, and the Big Meadows Horse Camp and Jack Lake Trailhead campsites were neat and clean. It was a memorable visit. Thanks to the Forest Service for a job well done! Keep stock at least 200' away from water sources.

Giddy-up!

Important notes: Use Oregon Wilderness map and GTM in this area. GTM 589 Three Fingered Jack will possibly be available the latter part of 1997. The Forest Service has been working with GTM to update their trails, by using the four digit numbers for areas east of the Cascades in the Jefferson Wilderness.

Mt. Jefferson Wilderness Index	Trail #
Bear Valley (to Minto Tie)	4006 (GTM Trail 83)
Big Meadows	3456
Blue Lake	3422
Booth Lake (Jack Lake to Square Lake)	4014
Bowerman Lakes	3492
Dixie Lakes	3494
Duffy Lake	3427
Marion Lake (north shore)	3436
Marion Lake Outlet	3495
Minto Pass	3437
Minto Tie	4006
Pacific Crest Tie	4015 (GTM 65A)
Pacific Crest Trail (PCT Tie to Bear Valley)	2000
Pine Ridge	3443
Wasco Lake (Jack Lake to Minto Pass)	4014 (GTM 65)

MOUNT JEFFERSON

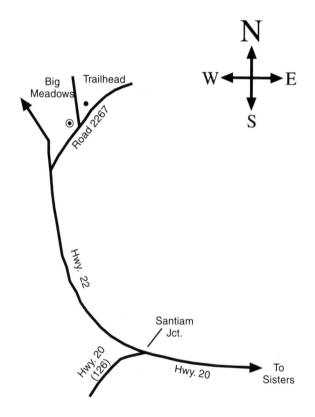

Big
Meadows

Trailhead

Road 2267

N

W ← → E

S

Hwy. 22

Santiam
Jct.

Hwy. 20
(126)

Hwy. 20

To
Sisters

• Trailhead

◉ Camping

Map not to scale

MOUNT JEFFERSON

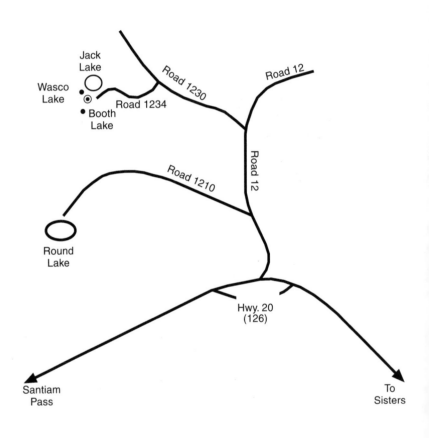

Jack Lake

Wasco Lake

Road 1230

Road 12

Road 1234

Booth Lake

Road 1210

Road 12

Round Lake

Hwy. 20 (126)

Santiam Pass

To Sisters

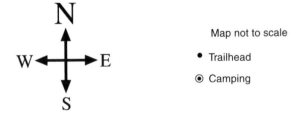

N

W   E

S

Map not to scale

• Trailhead

◉ Camping

Bear Valley #4006 (GTM 83)
(to Minto Tie)

Length:	3 miles
Elevation:	4800'-6300'
Map:	Mt. Jefferson Wilderness
	GTM 557 - Mt. Jefferson
Rating:	Easy-Medium (climbing)

Trailhead Directions: No trailhead.

Other Trails Accessed: 4006, 4005, 2000

Trail: Beginning from Rock Pile Lake on the PCT #2000, Bear Valley Trail starts at 6300'. The trail switchbacks down .5 mile, where Trail #70 (abandoned) intersects, going east. The trail levels out through the Windy Lakes area. This was a dusty and fun section of trail. As we looked back up at the ridge, it was amazing how high and rugged it looked from below. Bear Valley Trail connects with Minto Tie Trail at 4800'.

*Minto Tie Trail is not on the GTM.

*GTM lists Bear Valley Trail as being #83 and Two Springs (not maintained) as being #70.

Big Meadows #3456

Length:	2.4 miles
Elevation:	3600'-4400'
Map:	Mt. Jefferson Wilderness GTM 557 Mt. Jefferson GTM 589 Three Fingered Jack
Rating:	Easy

Trailhead Directions: Drive Highway 20 from Sisters, going west. It becomes Highway 22 at the Santiam Junction. In 4.5 miles, turn right on Road 2267 and drive 1.5 miles. Stay left on Road 2257 for .5 mile to Big Meadows Horse Camp and the trailhead.

Other Trails Accessed: 3427

Camping: Big Meadows Horse Camp offers 8 sites, water and corrals with nice fire pits and outhouses. There is a fee charged for this camp, you should arrive early. Day parking is available.

Trail: Big Meadows Trail begins east of Big Meadows Horse Camp at 3600'. The trail starts climbing gradually under towering timber; at 1.5 miles, Trail #3427 joins. The next short section of trail is flat and easy and takes you by a small pond in the lush forest. It parallels the Duffy Lake Trail. This trail used to be a connecting trail for Turpentine Trail (which is now closed).

Blue Lake #3422

Length:	7.6 miles
Elevation:	4000'-5200'
Map:	Mt. Jefferson Wilderness GTM 557 Mt. Jefferson
Rating:	Easy

Trailhead Directions: No trailhead.

Other Trails Accessed: 3491, 3494, 3443, 3495, 3436

Trail: Blue Lake Trail #3422 starts at Duffy lake and heads northeast to the vast Marion Lake. The trail goes past Mowich Lake, on the left. At 1.8 miles, Dixie Lakes Trail connects to your right. Riding north, you'll intersect Bowerman Lake Trail; then after 3 miles more of rolling hills, Pine Ridge Trail leaves going west. Connecting with Marion Lake Outlet, the Blue Lake Trail goes to the right down to Marion Lakes shore. This trail offers so many lakes that Josie got tired of pulling out maps, trying to identify them all! Excellent footing and scenery. Josie found Chicken of the Woods mushrooms and sautéed them in butter for dinner. YUMM!

Booth Lake #4014
(Jack Lake to Square Lake)

Length:	5.6 miles
Elevation:	4800'-5200'
Map:	Mt. Jefferson Wilderness GTM 589 Three Fingered Jack
Rating:	Easy

Trailhead Directions: From Sisters, take Highway 20 west (approximately 13 miles) and turn right on Road 12, turn left on Road 1230, then left on Road 1234. Follow this steep and washboard like road to its end and the trailhead.

Other Trails Accessed: 4012

Camping: Jack Lake Trailhead has 4 camp spots with tables, outhouse, and 4 horse corrals. Bring potable water; stock water is nearby. Store your food in trees or bear-proof containers.

Trail: The Booth Lake Trail #4014 is an easy ride from Jack Lake to Square Lake and has a wide variety of terrain. You'll encounter inclines and declines, forest, meadows, lakes, and streams. (The view of Three Finger Jack is awesome.) This trail was used to stretch out the horses after a 25 mile ride the previous day.

Josie and Madeleine near Three Fingered Jack

Bowerman Lakes #3492

Length:	3.3 miles
Elevation:	4700'-5200'
Map:	Mt. Jefferson Wilderness GTM 557 Mt. Jefferson
Rating:	Easy

Trailhead Directions: No trailhead.

Other Trails Accessed: 3437, 3422

Trail: Bowerman Lakes Trail #3492 connects Blue Lakes Trail and Minto Pass Trail. There is only a 500' elevation change. It is an interesting trail through the Eight Lakes Basin area. This is a beautiful trail through the forest with waist-high bushes. Josie and some friends found several miles of huckleberries that tempted their late-afternoon grumbling stomachs and WASPS! Loops are possible.

Dixie Lake #3494

Length:	1.5 miles
Elevation:	5200'
Map:	Mt. Jefferson Wilderness GTM 589 Three Fingered Jack GTM 557 Mt. Jefferson
Rating:	Easy

Trailhead Directions: No trailhead.

Other Trails Accessed: 3422, 3491

Trail: Dixie Lake Trail is mostly flat and runs by the North and South Dixie Lakes. It connects to Santiam Lake Trail #3491, and Blue Lake Trail #3422.

Duffy Lake #3427

Length:	3.5 miles
Elevation:	4000'-4800'
Map:	Mt. Jefferson Wilderness GTM 589 Three Fingered jack
Rating:	Easy

Trailhead Directions: No trailhead.

Other Trails Accessed: 3456, 3422, 3433, 3491

Trail: Duffy Lake Trail #3427 leaves Trail #3456 and climbs east, then levels off with good footing to the junction with Lava Trail #3433 and then Trail #3491. Duffy Lake is on the left at the end of the trail. Many loops are possible from here.

Marion Lake #3436
(north shore)

Length:	.8 miles
Elevation:	4000'-4100'
Map:	Mt. Jefferson Wilderness GTM 557 Mt. Jefferson
Rating:	Easy

Trailhead Directions: No trailhead.

Other Trails Accessed: 3495, 3437, 3422, 3493

Trail: This section of Marion Lake Trail starts at the "Y" intersection, with Trails #3437 from the southeast and #3493 going northeast. At .5 mile, Blue Lake Trail goes along the shore. Marion Lake Trail leaves the shore to go around a small hill. This brings you to the Marion Lake Outlet Trail #3495 at 4000'. This short section is used to complete loops in the area.

Marion Lake Outlet #3495

Length:	.8 miles
Elevation:	4000'-4100'
Map:	Mt. Jefferson Wilderness GTM 557 Mt. Jefferson
Rating:	Easy

Trailhead Directions: No trailhead.

Other Trails Accessed: 3422, 3436

Trail: Marion Lake Outlet Trail #3495 is only .8 mile long and goes through thick forest beginning at 4000'. It is used to make loops in this area.

Josie at Marion Lake

Minto Pass #3437

Length:	4.7 miles
Elevation:	4100'-5300'
Map:	Mt. Jefferson Wilderness GTM 557 Mt. Jefferson
Rating:	Easy-Medium (climbing)

Trailhead Directions: No trailhead.

Other Trails Accessed: 2000, 3492, 3493, 3436, 4015 (GTM 65A)

Trail: Minto Pass Trail starts at 5300' at a 3-way intersection with the PCT #2000 and Trail #4015. Begin down a gentle grade into meadows with sparse trees. The trail gradually gets steeper and deeper into the forest. At 2.7 miles, it joins with Bowerman Lake Trail #3492. The last 2 miles contours the hillside and passes cascading waterfalls. You'll cross a long bridge, which looks like a boardwalk, then arrive at the large Marion Lake at 4100', where the trail ends. Trail #3493 connects north and #3436 continues northwest. The ferns on this ride were over Josie's head and the forest floor was so old, it looked like the inside of a Butterfinger candy bar!

Josie near Minto Pass

Minto Tie #4006

Length:	1 mile
Elevation:	4600'-5200'
Map:	Mt. Jefferson Wilderness
Rating:	Medium

Trailhead Directions: No trailhead.

Other Trails Accessed: 4014, 4006

Trail: Minto Tie Trail starts from Bear Valley Trail #4006 at 4600', switchbacks up 600', then levels out on a boulder-sprinkled hillside. It intersects with Trail #4014 at the end of the trail.

*Trail #83 is #4006 on the Jefferson Wilderness Map.
*Trail #65 is #4014 on the Jefferson Wilderness Map.
*Minto Tie Trail is not on GTM.
*The new GTM will have updated 4 digit numbers.

Pacific Crest Tie #4015 (GTM 65A)

Length:	One quarter mile
Elevation:	5200'-5300'
Map:	Mt. Jefferson Wilderness GTM 557 Mt. Jefferson
Rating:	Medium-Hard (steep, rocky)

Trailhead Directions: No trailhead.

Other Trails Accessed: 2000, 4014 (GTM 65), 3437

Trail: Pacific Crest Tie Trail begins at 5200' from Wasco Lake Trail by Wasco Lake. It climbs steeply through a rockslide, emerging out on top of Minto Pass at 5300' and the end of the trail. Here you join the PCT #2000, going north and south, and #3437, going northwest, crossing the PCT.

Pacific Crest Trail #2000
(PCT Tie to Bear Valley)

Length:	3.5 miles
Elevation:	5300'-6300'
Map:	Mt. Jefferson Wilderness GTM 557 Mt. Jefferson
Rating:	Medium

Trailhead Directions: No trailhead.

Other Trails Accessed: 4015 (GTM 65A), 3437, 4006 (GTM 83)

Trail: This portion of the PCT #2000 heads north from Minto Pass, climbing steadily. It is a narrow trail on mostly open ridges. You'll arrive at a small meadow at Rockpile Lake at 6300'. Here it connects with Bear Valley Trail descending to the southeast.

Pine Ridge #3443

Length:	4.4 miles
Elevation:	4400'-4900'
Map:	Mt. Jefferson Wilderness GTM 557 Mt. Jefferson
Rating:	Easy

Trailhead Directions: Drive Highway 20 west from Sisters. It becomes Highway 22 after the Santiam Junction. Turn right on Road 2261 to the end of the road and Camp Pioneer. Roadside parking only.

Other Trails Accessed: 3422, 3435, 3444

Trail: Josie rode Pine Ridge Trail from the east to the west, beginning at Blue Lake Trail #3422. It begins at 4700', then intersects with Trail #3435 at 1 mile. The next 1.2 miles brings you to the intersection of Trail #3444; then in 2 miles more, you'll pass some small lakes, finally arriving at Camp Pioneer, where the trail ends. This trail can be dry and dusty, and has excellent footing.

Wasco Lake #4014 (GTM #65)
(Jack Lake to Minto Pass)

Length:	3.4 miles
Elevation:	5200'-5600'
Map:	Mt. Jefferson Wilderness
	GTM 557 Mt. Jefferson
	GTM 589 Three Fingered Jack
Rating:	Easy

Trailhead Directions: Drive Highway 20 west from Sisters and turn right on Road 12 (approximately 13 miles). Turn left on Road 1230 and left again on Road 1234, approximately 4.5 miles, then to the end of the steep and bumpy road at Jack Lake.

Other Trails Accessed: 4010, 4015 (GTM 65A), 2000, 4006

Camping: Jack Lake Trailhead has camping with several sites among the trees. Also available are 4 corrals and an outhouse. There are 3 campfire areas with tables. Bring potable water. Stock water is at the lake, to the north of the parking area. This is a no fee camp.

Trail: Wasco Lake Trail going to Minto pass starts on the southeast side of Jack Lake, horseshoeing around it to the north then west. This is a gentle, fun trail, that's well traveled. You'll join Trail #4010 at 1 mile, then enjoy numerous lakes. Ride by a rock slide; then pass Trail #4015 and Minto Tie Trail. In 1 mile more, the trail ends at 5600' on the PCT #2000. The trip is entirely in forest.

Jack Lake Camp

Oregon: Three Sisters Wilderness

The Three Sisters Wilderness area shows the same care and grooming of trails as the Jefferson Wilderness area. Josie was totally impressed. This area has rolling mountains with sandy soil and lava rocks. The views of the Three Sisters are breathtaking. (The mountains' names are Faith, Hope and Charity.) There are quite a number of other mountains that keep a constant vigil on you as you ride the many loops available. Oregon provides clean campgrounds; it is a grand vacation area to consider. The nearby resort at Crane Prairie has pay showers; Cultus Resort has a restaurant. Yeah! Store all food in bear-proof containers or use a food hoist. Keep all stock at least 200' from water sources.

*Important note: Use Oregon Three Sisters Map for this area.

Three Sisters Wilderness Index	Trail #
Cultus Butte	Road Ride
Metolius Windigo (south from Sisters Cow Camp)	99
North Cultus Lake Shelter Loop	16, 2000, 33
Sister Mirror Lake Loop	12, 20,2, 2000
Tam McArthur Rim	4078
West Cultus Lake	16, 15, 6
Wickiup Plains Loop	12, 20, 2000,
(to Racetrack Meadows)	3511, 3546, 3547

Sisters Cow Camp

Trail Notes

_____

_____

_____

_____

_____

_____

_____

_____

_____

_____

_____

THREE SISTERS

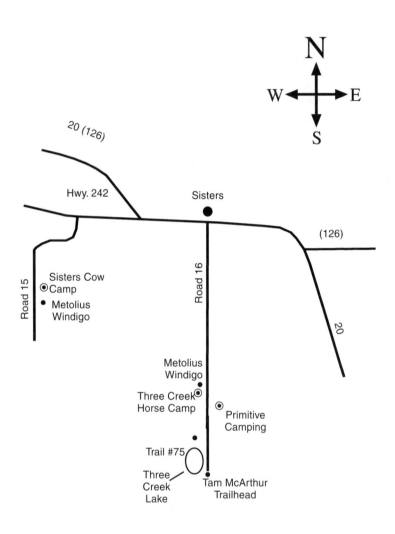

N

W ←→ E

S

20 (126)

Hwy. 242

Sisters

(126)

Road 15

Sisters Cow
⊙ Camp

● Metolius
Windigo

Road 16

20

Metolius
Windigo

Three Creek ⊙
Horse Camp

⊙
Primitive
Camping

Trail #75

Three
Creek
Lake

Tam McArthur
Trailhead

Map not to scale.

● Trailhead

⊙ Camping

THREE SISTERS

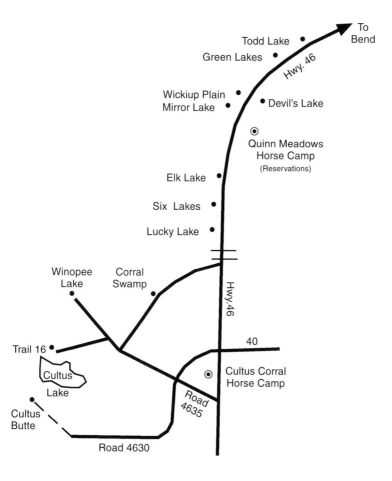

Todd Lake
Green Lakes
Hwy. 46
To Bend

Wickiup Plain
Mirror Lake
Devil's Lake

Quinn Meadows
Horse Camp
(Reservations)

Elk Lake

Six Lakes

Lucky Lake

Winopee
Lake
Corral
Swamp
Hwy. 46

Trail 16
40

Cultus Corral
Horse Camp

Cultus
Lake
Road 4635

Cultus
Butte

Road 4630

N
W ↔ E
S

• Trailhead

◉ Camping

Map not to scale

203

Cultus Butte
(road ride)

Length:	7.5 miles
Elevation:	4500'-6759'
Map:	Three Sisters Wilderness
Rating:	Medium

Trailhead Directions: Drive Cascade Lakes Highway 46 west out of Bend 40 miles. Go 4 miles south of Deschutes Bridge and go right on Road 4630. The Cultus Corral Horse Camp is 1 mile more on your left.

Camping: Cultus Corral is a big area, holding up to 200 people. It has 12 campsites, a nice outhouse, fire rings, shelter and 4 corrals for each campsite. There is a well, where you can pump water. A fee is required at this camp.

Trail: Cultus Butte road ride starts at Cultus Corral, taking Road 4630 to Little Cultus Lake. It curves around towards the north and follows an old logging road to the top. It's quite a climb up to 6759'. (Little Cultus Lake is at 4800'.) We included this ride because it was fun. Josie and friends watched the sun set from the top of the butte. It got dark as they were riding back, though they were able to see Crane Prairie and far-off Mount Shasta! The moon was full and it was a wonderfully warm evening to be with good friends as they returned to build a campfire.

Josie and Lady at Cultus Lake (Cultus Butte in background.)

Metolius Windigo #99

(South from Sisters Cow Camp)

Length:	7 miles
Elevation:	3200'-3600'
Map:	Three Sisters Wilderness
Rating:	Easy

Trailhead Directions: From Sisters, go west on Highway 242 and turn south onto Pole Creek Road 15. Go 2 miles and turn left on a dirt road. This is a historical site, since 1920, for rounding up sheep and cattle. It is well signed. No fee is required.

Other Trails Accessed: None.

Camping: Sisters Cow Camp has 4 big corrals, loading chutes, water troughs, and an outhouse. You need to bring potable water. The camp is in tall ponderosa timber. Picnic tables and fire pits are available. This is a spacious camp, and no fee is charged.

Trail: This section of Metolius Windigo Trail #99 leaves Sisters Cow Camp, heading south. The entire section of trail is easy, with good footing. This is an excellent warm-up trail or an easy trail for stretching out the stock after long rides. It is fairly flat, rolls along, and crosses several creeks. (Total mileage of the Metolius Windigo Trail runs 39 miles.)

Metolius
Windigo
Trail

North Cultus Lake Shelter Loop
(Trails: 16, 2000, 33)

Length:	20 miles
Elevation:	4635'-5200'
Map:	Three Sisters Wilderness
Rating:	Easy

Trailhead Directions: Drive Cascade Lakes Highway 46 out of Bend for 40 miles. Go 4 miles south of Deschutes Bridge and take a right on Road 4630. Cultus Corral is on the left 1 mile further. The trailhead is approximately 3 miles from Cultus Corral. Go past Cultus Corral, turn right on Road 4335, pass the Cultus Lake Resort turnoff, and continue straight ahead. The trailhead starts where the road ends. There is roadside parking only.

Other Trails Accessed: 8, 6

Camping: Cultus Corral has well water and room for 200 people and 30 horses. A fee is required. There are 12 sites, tables, fire rings, shelter and an outhouse.

Trail: North Cultus Lake Shelter Loop begins on the north shore of Cultus Lake. Trail #16 follows the rim of this huge sparkling lake for 2.6 miles. This section is wide and sandy. Within the next .5 mile Trail #8 exits to the north. As Trail #6 joins, continue on Trail #16 to the north. Just after the wilderness check-in point, Teddy Lakes Trail exits. Continue on Trail #16, passing Muskrat Lake, which is surrounded by deep swamp grass, with a view of the shelter across the far end. The next 2.7 miles is through open forest with excellent footing, which Josie loved! You'll meet Trail #33 at Winopee Lake. Stay on Trail #16 for 2 miles more, and climb gradually to the PCT #2000 for a great lunch spot. Turn right and ride to intersect Trail #33. Turn right again and head back with lakes all around you. It's a short 2 miles back to Trail #16; retrace your hoof prints back to the trailhead. There can be lots of mosquitos in June-July. The north shore of Cultus Lake Trail #16 is open to bicyclists, be aware.

Muskrat Lake History

A trapper built this cabin to take out muskrats sometime in the 1930's. Mink came down from the Mink Lake area and ate all the muskrats.

Josie

Muskrat Lake

Sister Mirror Lake Loop
(Trails: 12, 20, 2, 2000)

Length:	9.5 miles
Elevation:	5200'-6520'
Map:	Three Sisters Wilderness
Rating:	Easy

Trailhead Directions: Drive Cascade Lakes Highway 46, 30 miles from Bend. (The trailhead can be accessed from inside the locked gate, if you are staying at Quinn Meadows Horse Camp.) Park by the trailhead on the roadside. The trailhead is 3 miles past Devil's Lake and leaves from the west side of the road.

Other Trails Accessed: 3516, 3515

Camping: Quinn Meadows Horse Camp has 22 sites with 4 stalls to each site. There is well water, tables, fire pits, stock water, shelter, and an outhouse. It is a reservation system camp, so call far in advance. While staying here, we met Mounted Wilderness Ranger, Jim Leep, who brought in his mules and gave an informative talk about trails. Bring garbage bags, as you are required to move your stock's droppings away to the dump area. A fee is charged.

Trail: To start Sister Mirror Lake Loop, begin on the west side of Road 46 (from Quinn Meadows via an underpass). Turn left on a wide and sandy Trail #12 and parallel the road. Go right on Trail #2 for 1.6 miles; then take a right on the PCT #2000 for 4.3 miles, climbing up and over Koosah Mountain at 6520'. As you drop off the other side, the trail narrows, then flattens out. Sister Mirror Lake is in sight in a picturesque setting, so get out the camera! Keep your stock at least 200' away from the lake, as this is a heavily used area. Ride back on Trail #20, passing through lava pits. Turn right on Trail #12 and head back to camp, break out the "vittles," and RELAX! This is a real interesting ride!

Josie and Lady

Tam McArthur Rim #4078

Length:	3.5 miles
Elevation:	6800'-7600'
Map:	Three Sisters Wilderness
Rating:	Medium-Hard (climbing)

Trailhead Directions: From Sisters, drive Road 16 south. It is paved and steep for 13 miles, then levels out for the last 3 miles on a gravel road. The trailhead is on the south shore of Three Creek Lake.

Other Trails Accessed: None.

Camping: Three Creek Meadow Horse Camp has outhouses, corral stalls, tables, and fire pits. A fee is charged. There is stock water in the creek.

Trail: Tam McArthur Rim Trail begins at 6800' with climbing switchbacks. It levels out, then climbs again on a steep long grade. The last few miles are on an open ridge with the high point of this ridge at 7800'. The views make this trail a must-see area. Broken Hand, Three Sisters and Bachelor Butte are all at the end of your nose! Take the side trails to the rim to view the lakes below; it's incredible! The late lingering snow makes for awesome scenery.

The Three Sisters

West Cultus Lake

(Trails: 16, 15, 6)

Length:	10 miles
Elevation:	4635'-5200'
Map:	Three Sisters Wilderness
Rating:	Easy

Trailhead Directions: Drive Cascade Lakes Highway 46 out of Bend for 40 miles. Go 4 miles south of Deschutes Bridge and take a right on Road 4630. Cultus Corral is on the left 1 mile further. The trailhead is approximately 3 miles from camp. Go past Cultus Corral, turn right on Road 4335, pass the Cultus Lake Resort turnoff, and continue straight ahead. The trailhead starts where the road ends. There is roadside parking only.

Other Trails Accessed: 8

Camping: Cultus Corral has well water and room for 200 people and 30 horses. A fee is required. There are 12 sites, tables, fire rings, shelter and an outhouse.

Trail: West Cultus Lake ride starts with Trail #16, going west along the north shore of Cultus Lake. (Great views of Cultus Butte.) The trail is open, wide and well traveled. You'll join Trail #8, then Trail #6. Ride Trail #6; then turn right on Many Lakes Trail #15. Winding between numerous lakes, which feed each other, you'll reach the end of the trail at Road 600. This area etched a spot in Josie's mind, for the layout of the lakes is spectacular! This trail is an easy ride in the forest. Use caution on the north shore of Cultus Lake Trail #16, it's open to bicyclists.

Wickiup Plains Loop (to Racetrack Meadows)
(Trails: 12, 20, 2000, 3511, 3546, 3547)

Length:	26 miles
Elevation:	5300'-6400'
Map:	Three Sisters Wilderness
Rating:	Medium

Trailhead Directions: Take the Cascade Highway 46, 30 miles from Bend; the trailhead for Devil's Lake is on the left behind some trees.

Other Trails Accessed: 36, 13, 3527, 3547.1, 4331, 3524

Camping: Primitive camping with an outhouse is available at the small paved trailhead. No fee is charged. Josie and friends camped at Cultus Corral, 15 miles south of here. Quinn Meadows Horse Camp is also just down the road.

Ahhh, A Wickiup!
A wickiup is a shelter which is circular in shape. They were constructed with stout pine poles for support with smaller poles around covered with skins or woven mats. According to Volcanic Vistas newspaper, Wickiups have been dated to at least 9500 years old.

Josie

Trail: Wickiup Plain Loop starts with Trail #12 from Devil's Lake Trailhead. Go under the road, via an underpass. Ride on sandy footing through the forest and take Trail #12A to the PCT #2000; turn north (approximately 4 miles). Heading through Wickiup Plain, you get the feeling of being on the moon! The lava flow beds are enormous. The south Sister, Bachelor Butte, and Broken Top are in view. At the next intersection with Trail #3446, in deep forest, continue on the PCT #2000 for 4.2 miles more. Now you can see the Middle Sister as you near the junction of Racetrack Meadow Trail #3511, which you ride to the left. This area has terraced meadows with water running down the grass. At the next intersection of trails, stay to the far left on Trail #3546. Ride passing the James Creek Shelter, to intersect with the PCT #2000. Turn right to return to camp. This was a very enjoyable trail.

*The Three Sisters Wilderness Map shows the trail past James Creek Shelter on the front of the map as #3547. The back shows it as #3546.

Wickiup Plains Loop

Josie

Terri

Happy and safe trails!
Josie and Rene

Index

213

Trail Number Index